MAKING THE GRADE

MAKING THE GRADE

THE ACADEMIC SIDE OF COLLEGE LIFE

HOWARD S. BECKER
NORTHWESTERN UNIVERSITY

BLANCHE GEER
NORTHEASTERN UNIVERSITY

EVERETT C. HUGHES
BRANDEIS UNIVERSITY

JOHN WILEY AND SONS, INC.

NEW YORK · LONDON · SYDNEY · TORONTO

Library of Congress Catalog Card Number: 68-28498
SBN 471 06127 1
Printed in the United States of America

ACKNOWLEDGMENTS

After we completed (in collaboration with Anselm Strauss) the study of a medical school reported in *Boys in White,* we began the present study of the undergraduate college of the University of Kansas. Both theoretically and practically, it seemed a sensible next step. We were encouraged in this view by George Waggoner, the Dean of the College of Liberal Arts and Sciences of the University, who made us welcome and gave freely of his time, counsel, and criticism. We are greatly indebted to him for his help and for the critical discussions with him in which we tested and revised our ideas. Dean Waggoner read and commented on several versions of the manuscript; we have not always been able to use his criticisms, but we are grateful for all of them.

The Carnegie Corporation of New York provided financial support for the study and we thank them both for their support and for their patience in awaiting the final product.

Becker and Geer were employees of Community Studies, Inc., of Kansas City, Missouri, during the period of the research and the beginning of the analysis. We are grateful to W. D. Bryant, then Director of Community Studies, for his faith in us and for the superb working conditions he provided for us.

Marsh Ray was a member of the project staff for two years, during which time he did fieldwork on the Kansas campus and participated in project discussions. We have made much use of his work in this book.

Dorothy Seelinger and Kathryn Stoops typed the several thousand pages of field notes and memoranda we produced during the fieldwork phase of the project, as well as the first version of the manuscript. Lynne Johnson and Margaret Kimball typed other versions, and the final copy was produced by Patricia Hess and co-workers.

We wish to thank, finally, the many KU students who accepted us and helped us find out what we wanted to know and the many faculty members who allowed us to visit their classes.

CONTENTS

CONTENTS

LIST OF TABLES

CHAPTER 1

STUDYING COLLEGE STUDENTS:
THE NATURE OF OUR PROBLEM

What is it like to be a college student? Most of the people who read this book will have had the experience themselves, yet (unless they are very unusual) their memories will be dim and spotty. A few high points stand out, perhaps: a favorite professor, an exciting idea, a political triumph, a young romance. But the everyday experience of college—the background against which these emerge—will have faded beyond recall.

It is because we cannot remember our own college lives, perhaps, that we find it so difficult to understand and deal with college students. For we do find it difficult. Everyone recognizes how little we understand them when they flare up in what appear (to the outsider) to be irrational mass protests. Fewer people realize how much of the failure to achieve the educational goals colleges set for themselves results from the same lack of understanding. Still fewer see that, after all, students do make a life for themselves in college and that the kind of life they create is the most immediate influence on them; what teachers and administrators do influences them only as it is filtered through the network of their own culture and social arrangements.

Everyone writes about college students. Many people have studied them. Yet in all the vast literature that has accumulated we find very little that gives any sense of either the overall dimensions of college life, as students see them, or of the ordinary, routine everyday character it has for them. We can learn, from the literature, a great deal about the psychological and social characteristics of students: their personality traits, their attitudes on a variety of subjects, their social class, religion, and ethnicity. We can learn how these attributes are related to one another and how, taken singly or in combination, they correlate with stu-

1

dents' academic performance in school and their adjustment in later life. But we will not learn much about what they do, how they feel about it, what they think they are doing and why.[1]

Well, why should we? In a way, the volume that follows is our answer to that question, for we think that the analysis it presents will show what is to be gained from knowing college life as students see it. But, to answer briefly here, we should study students' views of their own experience because, we think, it is the best way to find out what influences those features of student behavior we are interested in. If we do not see it as they do—as a dense network of social relationships, institutional demands and constraints, and temporally connected contingencies—we will not be able to understand what they do.

We began our study of undergraduate life at the University of Kansas with that conviction, and our experience during the time we gathered and analyzed our data strengthened it. It has led us to organize our report in the way we have. Students typically divide college life into three major areas, and we have made these three the main foci of our work. First, they see the area of academic work: courses, grades, readings, term papers, examinations, and all the other paraphernalia that surround the college's core work of educating students. Second, they see an important area that revolves around campus organizations (both residential and "extracurricular") and campus politics. Finally, they recognize as a

---

[1] The literature on college students is voluminous, and it would be pointless to document fully these blanket assertions. A variety of approaches are contained in R. Nevitt Sanford, *The American College* (New York: John Wiley and Sons, 1962). Other important works are: Theodore M. Newcomb and Everett K. Wilson, eds., *College Peer Groups* (Chicago: Aldine Publishing Co., 1966); Esther Raushenbush, *The Student and His Studies* (Middletown, Conn.: Wesleyan University Press, 1964); Rose K. Goldsen et al., *What College Students Think* (Princeton, N.J.: Van Nostrand, 1960). Theodore M. Newcomb, *Personality and Social Change* (New York: Holt, Rinehart and Winston, 1943); W. A. Scott, *Values and Organizations: A Study of Fraternities and Sororities* (Chicago: Rand McNally & Co., 1965); David Boroff, *Campus U.S.A.* (New York, Harper and Bros., 1958); Bryant M. Wedge, ed., *Psychosocial Problems of College Men* (New Haven, Conn.: Yale University Press, 1958); Philip Jacob, *Changing Values in College* (New Haven, Conn.: Edward W. Hazen Foundation, 1957); Edward D. Eddy, Jr., *The College Influence on Student Character* (Washington, D.C.: American Council on Education, 1959); Leila Sussman, *Freshman Morale at M.I.T.* (Cambridge, Mass.: Massachusetts Institute of Technology, 1960); Walter L. Wallace, *Student Culture* (Chicago: Aldine Publishing Co., 1966); James S. Davie and A. Paul Hare, "Buttondown Collar Culture: A Study of Undergraduate Life at a Men's College," *Human Organization*, 14 (Winter, 1956), pp. 13–20; Rebecca S. Vreeland and Charles E. Bidwell, "Classifying University Departments: An Approach to the Analysis of Their Effects Upon Undergraduates' Values and Attitudes," *Sociology of Education*, 39 (Summer, 1966), pp. 237–354, and "Organizational Effects of Student Attitudes: A Study of the Harvard Houses," *ibid.*, 38 (Spring, 1965), pp. 233–250.

third area that of personal relationships, both friendships (usually same-sex) and those of dating and courtship.

We found, to our dismay, that the analysis and presentation of material on all three of these areas, desirable as it would be, cannot be achieved in one book-length report. It would be desirable because the three are linked in so many ways, both objectively and in the students' eyes; to present them separately makes it difficult to justify some aspects of the argument, which more properly belong in a place devoted particularly to that topic. Thus, we can hardly understand how students deal with their academic work without knowing something about its relation to campus politics. We have solved the problem by using the conclusions from one area of our study in the analysis of another, hoping that readers will tentatively accept those conclusions until they are given a full analysis of their own.[2]

Be that as it may, in this, the first volume to appear from our study, we concentrate on the academic side of student life and give relatively little attention to organizations, politics, and personal relations. We speak of these matters frequently, whenever some understanding of them is needed for our discussion of academic work, but their full analysis is delayed until later publications.

ACADEMIC WORK

Research on college students deals mainly with their academic performance but ordinarily takes a direction very different from ours. Most of this research has a little of the character of industrial research designed to improve the efficiency of some production process. It asks whether the educational job is getting done: Are students learning? How much? What things? It asks under what conditions the job is done best: In large classes or small? With lectures or discussions? Under what kinds of college organization? It asks how the character of the materials used affects the product: Do the intellectual, attitudinal, emotional, and social traits of students influence the efficiency of the educational process? Or, more subtly, does the combination of students of different kinds in one campus population influence the result?[3]

These are serious questions, of course. But they are teachers' questions

[2] Some preliminary statements about campus organizations can be found in Blanche Geer, "Student Government, The Fraternity System, and The University Administration," *Journal of the Association of Deans and Administrators of Student Affairs*, 3 (July, 1965), pp. 17–21, and in Howard S. Becker, "Student Culture," in Roy Ingham, ed., *The Dynamics of Change in the Modern University* (Boston: Center for the Study of Liberal Education for Adults, Boston University, 1966), pp. 59–80.

[3] See the studies cited in Footnote 1.

and administrators' questions. They are not the questions that suggest themselves for study if we look at academic work from the students' point of view. From that point of view, much that seems important to others becomes trivial and, conversely, what teachers and administrators think trivial comes to have much more importance.

We shall have so much occasion, in the course of this volume, to list the kinds of questions about academic work students are concerned with that, to avoid being tedious, we do not begin the listing here. Suffice it to say that they are questions of this general order: What is it that is asked of me in my academic work? What is it that I myself want of that work? How do I go about satisfying these demands? What will happen to me if I succeed, or if I fail to meet them?

Though we look at the area of academic work from the students' point of view, we do not simply ask their questions, providing perhaps a bit more rigor, breadth, or wisdom in the answers. We are, after all, sociologists, and we approach these questions as one aspect of the thing we are studying. We study people who spend some of their time asking themselves such questions, trying to answer them, and acting on the answers they achieve. Our job is to make sense of that phenomenon, and we do this by seeing it from our own, sociological perspective.

A SOCIOLOGICAL CONTEXT

So far we have spoken only of our *area of interest* in this volume—academic work—without specifying the *problem* that we, as social scientists, propose to study. An area of interest becomes a scientific problem when it is put into a theoretical context, and the kind of problem, obviously, is a function of the particular theoretical context used. Ours is sociological and, within that broad category, it is a theory based on the concept of symbolic interaction, as that can be found in the work of Dewey, Cooley, George Herbert Mead, Park, and others.

Mead begins his analysis of human conduct by noting that people have the ability to view their own behavior from the standpoint of another. They can imagine what their actions will be taken to mean by others and thus are able to organize what they do, even as it is being done, so as to take account of the anticipated responses of others. This is the import of "symbolic" in the term symbolic interaction, for actions acquire symbolic value as they achieve, through this mechanism of "role taking," the quality of having the same meaning to both the person who performs them and the person or persons with whom he is interacting. Insofar as the meanings of actions are in this fashion shared, and people organize their own activity with reference to those shared meanings, the possibility of collective action arises. Individual actions take shape as the person attempts to mesh what he does with what others around him are doing, so that the nature of the collective action he is participating in becomes a major explanation of what he does.[4]

Sociology, from one point of view, consists of the study of collective action: the forms it takes, the conditions under which they arise, and their consequences. In speaking of collective action, it should be clear that we do not refer to such instances of elementary collective behavior as the crowd or the mob, but rather to more stable forms of joint endeavor—what are usually referred to as institutions, organizations, or establishments. All social structures, after all, consist of a large number of people joining their various and differentiated lines of individual activity into some kind of coordinated collective activity.

Collective action takes place in an environment or situation, which is simply to say that it goes on under conditions set by the physical world and by the network of other forms of collective action in which it is embedded. Whatever the participants in the action may want to do, they are constrained to choose among those alternatives that the situation allows them. Collective action is thus a function both of the desires, individual and shared, of the actors and the conditions under which they act.

We use the concept of perspective to analyze the collective actions of relatively homogeneous groups—homogeneous with respect to their social position in an institution. We have elsewhere defined a perspective as

> . . . a coordinated set of ideas and actions a person uses in dealing with some problematic situation, . . . a person's ordinary way of thinking and feeling about and acting in such a situation. These thoughts and actions are coordinated in the sense that the actions flow reasonably, from the actor's perspective, from the ideas contained in the perspective. Similarly, the ideas can be seen by an observer to be one of the possible sets of ideas which might form the underlying rationale for the person's actions and are seen by the actor as providing a justification for acting as he does.[5]

Perspectives, though they are used by the individual to organize his activity, are a group phenomenon, coming into being when the members of a group find themselves sharing common or similar goals in a common situation. (We analyze the concept at greater length in Chapter 3.)

[4] See George Herbert Mead, *Mind, Self, and Society* (Chicago: University of Chicago Press, 1934), and Herbert Blumer, "Sociological Implications of the Thought of George Herbert Mead," *American Journal of Sociology*, 71 (March, 1966), pp. 535–544.
[5] Howard S. Becker, Blanche Geer, Everett C. Hughes, and Anselm L. Strauss, *Boys in White: Student Culture in Medical School* (Chicago: University of Chicago Press, 1961), p. 34.

The formula for our analysis, then, is that under given conditions, which we may expect to be largely socially created, groups work out collective modes of action or perspectives. We can thus transform our area of interest—academic work—into this scientific problem: What kinds of perspectives do college students create to deal with their academic work under the conditions of college life? The same formula will allow us, in later writings, to raise similar questions about the areas of organizations and politics and of friendship and dating.

CONDITIONS OF STUDENT ACTIVITY

We studied the forms of collective action found among students in a residential college. Since they live in a small college town, the college and its supporting institutions constitute the main setting for their lives as students. For the most part, what college authorities do structures their situation. These authorities—the faculty and administration—set the terms for a large portion, though not all, of student activity. They determine what students will be required to do and, similarly, what they will be allowed, though not required, or forbidden to do. They provide as well the resources available to students out of which and around which they can shape their collective action. That is, where they do not require or forbid behavior, they create the conditions in which that behavior will take place.

College authorities do not, of course, exercise as complete control over student life as they might. In some areas, students are free to escape the college and its surrounding town and go elsewhere for their activity. Furthermore, we do not imply that college authorities are free to set whatever terms or create whatever conditions they wish. They, too, are subject to social constraints and must work with the resources available to them. We have focused on the collective activities of students and the conditions under which they arise, but a similar study could easily be made of college authorities themselves. One point, in particular, needs to be noted: In some areas of student life, students become sufficiently well-organized and powerful to set for themselves the conditions under which college authorities act, so that, in some measure, students and authorities set the conditions for one another's action and constitute an important part of each other's environment.

We must distinguish two connected levels of analysis, both of which we make use of. We have just discussed the collective action students take in response to conditions created by others, by nonstudents. We also attend to individuals and student groups as they fashion their own lines of action, focusing on the constraints they exercise on one another's actions.

For example, we may analyze the fraternities as part of the collective response of students to the problems of finding a residence and organizing themselves for action in the conditions set by university authorities. But when we analyze dating or campus political activity, we must take the existence of fraternities and their characteristic activities as part of the conditions under which dating and political activity take *their* characteristic forms.

Although we concentrate in this book on the area of academic work, in the remainder of this chapter we consider the conditions of student action in all three areas of student activity. We do this because variation in the conditions surrounding each area of activity leads to differences in the student perspectives associated with those activities and, though we cannot complete the demonstration of that proposition in this volume, we want eventually to be able to do so and thus want to make the basis of the argument clear.

Academic Work

Faculty and administration set almost all the terms and conditions of student activity in the academic area; their control is here most nearly complete. They decide what students are to do, when they are to do it, something of how it is to be done, and what rewards or punishments will be given to those who do or do not meet the standards. The terms they set are largely contained in the system of courses, credits, examinations, and grades described in every university catalog. They are further contained in all the rules and regulations in which performance in the academic area is made a prerequisite for some other kind of activity or privilege.

The relation between students and university in this area may reasonably be called one of *subjection*. We must understand, of course, that the term does not express an unfavorable judgment. We use it as a technical term, to refer to a hierarchical arrangement in which all the decision-making power is in the hands of the superior group. The faculty, of course, believe, with a good deal of reason, that this is an appropriate pattern, since they, after all, know a good deal more about their subject matter than students do and so ought not to be expected to give up any power in this area. (This view has sometimes been challenged by students, as in the Berkeley affair.) Whatever the rights and wrongs of the matter, it is clear that in the academic area students are almost completely powerless. They may, as individuals, complain to a particular teacher about a particular assignment or grade. They may organize among themselves to deal with the demands made of them by the faculty. But whatever form their collective activity takes, it is a form greatly constrained by the requirements laid down by the university authorities.

The general conditions under which students act in the academic area are the same for everyone. Every student is subject to university regulations about courses, grades, and credits, and to all the subsidiary regulations that make use of these as criteria on which to base a decision about other areas of the student's life. The regulations, of course, affect different students differently. In particular, some students, either because of native ability or because of motivation or work habits, find it easier to meet the requirements than others. Similarly, some students and student groups are so placed in campus social structure that they have certain advantages with respect to academic work that are not available to other students. Nevertheless, the conditions affecting all students are very much alike, as we shall see, and we can reasonably expect them all to have a very similar and shared perspective on academic work. We expect, too, to find variations in detail and emphasis in this perspective that go along with the variations in ability to meet the requirements just noted. But even though there are variations, the perspective will provide a common basis of understanding for all students and common ground for coordinated action where the necessity arises.

We describe the conditions and constraints in the area of academic work in this volume, and go on to analyze in some detail the perspective students have developed—the kinds of collective understandings they acquire and the activities they engage in response to university demands. The chief feature of their perspective is an emphasis on grades as the chief reward to be gained and on methods of meeting faculty demands so as to achieve desired grade levels.[6]

Organizations and Politics

We have avoided speaking of extracurricular activities, though the term points adequately to what we mean, largely because students themselves do not think of these activities as quite so unimportant and trivial as faculty members usually do and as the term implies. In fact, they regard them as matters of major importance, often as more important than the academic work of the university. We prefer, following their lead, to think of this as the area of student organizations and politics.

The university exerts much less control over this area of student life than it does over academic work. It has left important areas of activity to the students to define and organize. It is not that the university exerts no control, for it does issue regulations, set the basic conditions under which

[6] Other studies have pointed to a similar emphasis on grades. See Wallace, *op. cit.*, and Sussman, *op. cit.*

student organizations can operate, and provide some of the facilities for student activity. Nevertheless, university authorities do not specify in much detail what students are to do and how they are to do it. Rather, they tell them what kind of thing ought to be done and make a few basic rules as to how activities are to be carried on, leaving many of the detailed decisions to students.

For example, the university has allowed students to develop their own housing, both cooperatives and, much more importantly, fraternities and sororities. Similarly, they have left such activities as student government and the organization of many recreational and service activities very much in the hands of students. Students, in short, have the opportunity to mobilize student activity in a great many areas in which the university desires some activity to take place, and without the constraint of overly detailed regulation of what they do.

Their control over residential and organizational matters gives students a great deal of power. For the university wants the things done that student organizations do. Though it may have built a great many dormitories, it finds the housing provided by fraternities and sororities useful. It finds useful, too, the kind of self-policing these organizations do. (The university staff handling such matters is quite small in comparison to the academic staff). It depends on the many kinds of work done by the student government and by the groups that run such activities as the Student Union and the campus newspaper.[7] Insofar as students have the option to do these things or not, and can choose whether to do them in a way the university approves, they have a great deal of power. Because they have power, university authorities are not free to set the terms of action for students unilaterally. Rather, authorities must negotiate and bargain with students to achieve a satisfactory adjustment. As opposed to the academic area, in which *subjection* seemed a reasonable term to apply to the relations of students and university authorities, we can characterize the relation here as one of *negotiation*.[8]

While the university benefits when students engage in such activities, it does not require of any particular student that he do so. Some become involved, others do not by their own choice. Insofar as there is a generalized student perspective about student organizations, it simply states that there is something here one can get into if he wants, but need not. The result is that some students are very involved and others not at all, with all shades between.

[7] Many other institutions, such as prisons and mental hospitals, depend on "client labor" to get their work done. See, for instance, Anselm Strauss et al., *Psychiatric Ideologies and Institutions* (New York: The Free Press, 1964), pp. 93–124.
[8] On the relation of negotiation and social structure, see *ibid.*, pp. 292–315.

Student perspectives reflect this differential involvement. A large number of students, only peripherally involved, have sketchy and vague perspectives with respect to student organizations. Other students, much more involved, spend most of their time in organizational activity. As might be expected, these students have developed a complicated and detailed perspective. They have, in addition, developed a network of organizations and patterns of acting together within those organizations.

While students involved in organizational activity by no means include the entire student body, neither are they a negligible fraction. The perspectives of involved students emphasize the uses to which their organizational power may be put, the role it plays in the activity of the total university, and the benefits they may individually gain from the experience of exercising it. They have organized themselves around these issues, developing working relationships among themselves and with university authorities.

The university, in short, not only sets the conditions for student activity in this area but also makes some of the rules. However, because it wants the products of that activity and because it has left large amounts of it unregulated and undefined, power has slipped into students' hands, and the result is a relationship of bargaining and negotiation between students and university authorities.

Personal Relations

In the area of dating and friendship, the university participates hardly at all, exerting control largely by setting the conditions of student activity in an almost ecological way. These activities are, in a real sense, only symbiotically attached to the university. The university does not require that any student have either friends or dates. Some university authorities, particularly the personnel deans, have a substantial interest in such matters. But the university does not assert the right to a legitimate voice in what a student does. It does, of course, make a few rules, but they are minimal, having largely to do with enforcing the typically Victorian notion, almost universal in American colleges, of protecting female virtue.

Perhaps the point can be made more clearly by saying that no authority requires any student to be a friend, a date, a lover, or a fiancé. The reader will remember that the university requires all students to operate effectively in the academic area and that it benefits greatly from students' organizational activities. It has no such interest in students' personal relations and could operate quite adequately if no students engaged in such activities.

Given the university attitude toward personal relations, students are free to build a way of life and a pattern of collective activity by themselves. They get no guidance from the university (only a minimal amount of regulation) and very little help, largely in the form of providing places in which such activities may be carried on. (The regulations, in addition to rules guarding female virtue, also help students to coordinate social activities by providing a common means of scheduling events.)

By virtue of being young Americans, students typically want friends and an opportunity to date and perhaps eventually to meet a marriageable person. But not all students share these desires and, perhaps more important, not all students feel it necessary to satisfy them within the university community. Thus, many students arrange their sex lives so as to revolve around someone who is not present on the campus, perhaps a girl back home or a boy in the armed services. There is room, too, for personal variation in desires. Some students have a great desire for close friends; others only want a few people they know just well enough to shop or drink beer with; still others are lone wolves. Some students, greatly concerned about meeting members of the opposite sex, devote a great deal of their time and effort to it; some want only to do what is conventionally done; others are social celibates. The university allows any of these adjustments and for all practical purposes is indifferent to the matter.[9]

In saying that the university is indifferent we do not imply that it is heartless and unfeeling. Rather, it is a matter of institutional legitimacy. The university (quite properly, we think) realizes that it has no legitimate right to interfere in students' personal relations, no right to require that one have friends or date. As an organization, it is officially indifferent, because the American ethos would hardly let it be otherwise; we regard these matters as properly belonging to the individual's own sphere of competence and decision.

So students build their own way of life and pattern of activity, constrained only by a very few university rules and making use of the resources available in the university and the environing community. What they build varies a great deal. Some take part in an elaborately organized system of dating, mediated by the structure of living groups. For these students, heterosexual relations are quite ritualized—a highly organized system of formal functions regulated by the students' own groups. Others depend on a loosely connected network of introductions and ac-

---

[9] Two interesting earlier studies are Willard Waller, "The Rating-Dating Complex," *American Sociological Review*, 2 (1937), pp. 727–734, and Winston W. Ehrmann, *Premarital Sex Behavior* (New York: Holt, Rinehart and Winston, 1959).

quaintances, making use of the ordinary recreational facilities available to all citizens of the university community. Still others find a simple dyadic relationship, which persists through college.

It is the same with respect to friendship. Some students have a great many friends, by virtue of belonging to certain organizations or living in a certain residential unit. Some students have a loose-knit network of friends and still others may have no friends at all, or at best a very few.

The loose control the university exercises over personal relations allows students to express a great variety of individual desires and patterns of activity. Free to do as they wish or as they can, their desires and activities are likely to be influenced more in this area than in any other by what they have brought with them, by their extrastudent identities and cultures.

The main difference is between men and women. Men take dating less seriously than women. For women, college dating is not a rehearsal, but the real thing. Most college girls hope or expect that during their time in college they will meet the man (or at least the kind of man) they will eventually marry. If they do not, they have already begun to pass the age at which it would be natural for them to do so, or so they think. So dating plays a much larger role in their lives as students than it does for men, affecting what they do in the academic and organizational areas as well to a far greater degree than men are affected.

Students differ in this area of activity not only in what they have brought with them, but also in what they get into once they arrive on campus. We refer here, of course, to the difference between members of fraternities and sororities and independent students. Fraternity men and sorority women have a great deal provided for them, by way of automatic introductions to friends and potential dates, that is denied to the independent. Their patterns of collective activity here are quite different.

In comparison with the pattern of subjection characteristic of academic relations of university and students and the pattern of negotiation in extracurricular affairs, we may speak in this area of a relationship of *indifference* between students and the university. The university does not desire to intervene and is officially indifferent (with a few exceptions) to what students do. Students do not expect the university to intervene (and might, in many cases, wish to do away with even those few exceptions).

A Restatement of Our Problem

In this volume, then, we will analyze the patterns of collective action students develop in their academic work, under the major condition of a relationship of subjection or unilateral authority with the college faculty and administration. We will thus enable ourselves to understand what the academic side of college life looks like to students and to understand as well how the environment they operate in constrains them to see things as they do. Our analysis should lead both to a deeper understanding of similar relationships in other kinds of social settings and to a more adequate conceptualization of some of the problems of college life conventionally studied by social scientists.

RESEARCH METHODS

We used the method of participant observation to study student perspectives. The method has been described in the literature, to which the reader can turn for a fuller account than we give here.[10] Briefly, it consists of observation conducted while participating, to a greater or lesser degree, in the lives of those studied. The participant observer follows those he studies through their daily round of life, seeing what they do, when, with whom, and under what circumstances, and querying them about the meaning of their actions. In this way, he builds up a body of field notes and interviews that come nearer than any other social science method to capturing patterns of collective action as they occur in real life.

In our study, three observers (Becker, Geer, and Ray) spent more than two years working with students at the University of Kansas. We went to classes with them, spent time with them in their residential units, attended formal and informal meetings of all kinds of campus organizations, and participated in many aspects of informal campus social life. We did not pretend to be students, nor did we assume any of the formal obligations of students; though we went to class with them, we did not do homework or take examinations. The nature of our fieldwork will become clear in the quotations from our field notes that appear throughout the book.

A fourth observer (Hughes) spent two semesters at the University as a visiting professor and in that capacity gathered data on the perspectives of faculty and administration. The other observers occasionally gathered similar material and, in addition, made extensive use of documents prepared by the administration and by other organizations, largely to characterize the environment in which students act.

Participant observation produces a large body of unsystematic material. We have described elsewhere our methods of analyzing such data

[10] See Buford H. Junker, *Field Work* (Chicago: University of Chicago Press, 1960), and Severyn Bruyn, *The Human Perspective in Sociology* (Englewood Cliffs, N.J.: Prentice-Hall, 1966).

and do not repeat that discussion here.[11] In this volume the analysis is relatively straightforward. We combed our field notes for all material bearing on the academic side of college life and developed generalizations about student perspectives and the conditions under which they appear that took account of all the available data; negative data are discussed in Chapter 9.

A word is in order regarding our use of quotations from field notes. These quotations serve several purposes. As already noted, they allow the reader to see how we carried on our field operations. In addition, they give him a "feel," beyond the formal analysis, for the quality of student concerns. They provide (because we tend to quote at length) a basis on which the reader may consider alternative formulations to the ones we have presented. Finally, they stand as examples of the kinds of items counted up as evidence for our analysis of student perspectives.

[11] Howard S. Becker and Blanche Geer, "Participant Observation: The Analysis of Qualitative Field Data," in Richard Adams and Jack J. Preiss, *Human Organization Research* (Homewood, Ill.: Dorsey Press, 1960), pp. 267–289; and Blanche Geer, "First Days in the Field," in Phillip E. Hammond, ed., *Sociologists at Work* (New York: Basic Books, 1964), pp. 322–344.

CHAPTER 2

THE UNIVERSITY OF KANSAS

We studied the perspectives students develop toward academic work in a particular place—the University of Kansas—and our readers will want to know some of the basic facts about the University before we proceed with our analysis. We present a selection of those facts here, to satisfy that curiosity and to allow readers to see where the University fits in their own picture of American higher education.

But we present them for another reason as well. The "basic facts" tell us something about the way the rest of the society—the social environment of the University—affects the University's operation. Other institutions, organizations, and groups ask and require things of the University; they furnish the personnel and other raw materials with which it works; they receive and judge its products; they provide financial support. The environment thus constrains and limits what can be done just as it opens up possibilities for what can be done.

The University, like all organizations, strives to achieve its ends in its environment. We should not be misled by this way of talking into thinking that the University as an entity has ends that it, again as an entity, pursues. Rather, different members of the University, participants in its doings at one level or another, have their own ends that they pursue, individually or collectively. It would be a mistake to think that the University operates only toward one goal. Its various members have multiple and diverse, possibly even contradictory, ends in view.

But whatever the ends the participants in the University strive to attain, these ends must be attained in its environmental context and must be in the range of what that context makes possible. The University thus arrives finally at some kind of adjustment to its environment. It develops practices, institutions, and customs which can be conceived as ways of dealing with the constraints of the outer world. It finds a *modus*

15

vivendi, a compromise or adjustment of the varying ends of participants in the organization to those constraints.

The adjustment the University makes to the rest of the world is important for our analysis because the character of that adjustment is translated, through the actions of University administrators, faculty, and other personnel, into constraints on students, on residential groups, and on other student organizations. This conception has guided our choice of facts to present, for we have proceeded by describing those aspects of University environment and its organizational response to that environment which exert an influence on student perspectives on academic work. We have slighted those areas—for example, the University's position of *in loco parentis* vis-à-vis students—that, however important they may be for other student activities, do not much influence academic perspectives.

We started our fieldwork in 1959 and completed it in 1961. The University has changed greatly in the interim, and it should be clear that the figures we present and the other organizational features we describe represent the University at that time. Some of the things we describe are characteristic of most American universities. Others are to be found only in certain kinds of universities, particularly the large state schools. Still others may be unique to Kansas. The generalizability of our analysis is problematic. We think it likely that much of what we describe in this volume is true of most state universities and, indeed, of most universities. But we argue only that where the conditions found at Kansas occur, the consequences are likely to be the same. We describe the conditions under which the University operates, leaving it to the reader to judge how typical of all undergraduate colleges these are.

LOCATION

The University (except for the medical school, which is located in Kansas City, Kansas) has its home in Lawrence, Kansas, a town of more than 32,000 (hence one of the largest cities in the state, exceeded in population only by the Kansas City suburban ring, Wichita, Topeka, and Salina). Downtown Kansas City is about forty-five minutes away by car, and Topeka less than that. Though the city has other industries, the University is its biggest business. Lawrence is a college town.

Situated in the rolling hills of the more heavily populated eastern third of the state, most of the University sits atop Mount Oread, a high hill that looks out across the plains to the hundreds of smaller cities and towns that make up its constituency. Bigger than most of them, Lawrence is something of a cultural and intellectual center for the state, despite the competition from Kansas City and Topeka (which has more of such amenities than its size warrants, because of its position as a world-famous center of psychiatric treatment and research).

Lawrence looks like a Midwestern college town. The University, with its old and new school buildings, its dormitories, fraternity and sorority houses, its football stadium, and its tree-lined streets filled with students, stands at the center. Beyond it lie the comfortable homes of the faculty and townspeople, and beyond that the suburban developments found around every American city. Just to the north, within walking distance, are downtown Lawrence, the shopping and business center, the Kaw River, and the Kansas Turnpike.

FACULTY

When the University first opened its doors in 1866, it had a faculty of three. In 1959, when we began our study, the faculty (excluding the professional faculties in medicine) consisted of 699 people, 354 of them in the College of Liberal Arts. (See Table 1.) Although Kansas cannot

TABLE 1
Faculty of the University of Kansas, 1959

	Professors	Associate professors	Assistant professors	Instructors [a]	Total
College of Liberal Arts	93	89	101	71	354
School of Business	7	6	11	4	28
School of Education	25	21	27	22	95
School of Engineering and Architecture	20	23	17	49	109
School of Fine Arts	16	18	19	19	72
School of Journalism	2	4	6	4	16
School of Law	5	3	3	0	11
School of Medicine	46	60	112	210	428
School of Pharmacy	3	1	1	2	7
R.O.T.C., etc.	3	3	12	0	18
Total	220	228	309	381	1138
College of Liberal Arts					
Humanities	25	28	28	37	118
Sciences	43	50	51	18	162
Social Sciences	25	11	22	16	74
Total	93	89	101	71	354

[a] Includes lecturers but not associates or assistant instructors.
Source: Announcement of Courses Bulletin, University of Kansas, 1959, pp. 315–381.

compete with such giants as California or with some of the leading private universities in the number of Nobel Prize winners among faculty members, it has a faculty with many outstanding men and departments.[1]

It is notoriously difficult to measure the quality of a faculty and we have not attempted that here. We can, however, point to Kansas' successful effort to recruit its faculty from the national pool of talent, rather than relying, as many schools do, on the nostalgia of those who have received their advanced degrees there. Three quarters of the faculty received no advanced degree from Kansas.

We can report, too, the feeling of University administrators that they have had more than their share of success in attracting and keeping first-rate faculty members. In this, they have carried on a tradition begun by Kansas' clergymen founders from New England, who modeled it on Harvard.

A distinguished faculty demands a great deal of academic achievement from students. They set high standards, assign large amounts of work, and expect students to complete the work at a level they consider adequate. Because it is possible for them to move to other universities, should anyone suggest that they lower their standards (an unlikely suggestion), they would leave rather than compromise.

RELATIONS WITH STATE AND SOCIETY

The University receives its mandate from the state, which charters it. This symbolizes the University's responsibility to the citizens of the state for the quality of the job it does. The University is a state institution, financed in large part by appropriations made by the State Legislature. A Board of Regents, appointed by the Governor, is the highest governing body of the University. The State Legislature periodically appropriates money for the University, as well as for other state institutions of higher education.

Because the Regents and the Legislature need information on which to base their judgments, and because the administration of the University itself needs information, the University may from one point of view be seen as a gigantic information-gathering and processing machine. It has offices that provide this information and officers whose main duty is to see that the appropriate kinds of information are available to all who need it. The necessary information may, for instance, simply consist of a report on the number of students of various kinds enrolled at the University. It may consist of financial information—on the costs of running the University and on the income available to meet those costs.

[1] Information on the faculty and history of the University are taken from *Announcement of Courses Bulletin,* University of Kansas, 1959.

One kind of information-gathering has special relevance for our later analysis. Almost every educational institution seems to find it necessary to have a system for assessing how well the institution is doing the job of inculcating learning into its students. Teachers sometimes feel that there is no really foolproof way of assessing how well students have learned what they are being taught. They occasionally protest against systems of examination and grading. The reasons for the continued existence of such systems of assessment would make a fascinating study. We have not made that study. Veblen, for instance, once suggested that such systems arose because the industrial leaders who really ran universities felt the need of some bureaucratically efficient measure of performance.[2] We need not accept Veblen's hypothesis to recognize that the question is meaningful and important.

Nevertheless, without answering the question why systems of examination and grading are found in universities, we can note their existence and report the results of its work in some objective way, but also from operation of the University.

We should not forget that systems of grading may have multiple origins. They may result not only from the desire of the university to assess and report the results of its work in some objective way, but also from the desire of teachers to know whether their students are learning anything. We should note, however, that this question could be answered without a university-wide system of grades, university rules about examinations, and such devices as the cumulative grade point average. Similarly, examinations and grades are used by those institutions who receive the students prepared by the university, as a way, for instance, of deciding which among them should be permitted to engage in further study. They could not do this unless there was an objective, university-wide system of examining. But in this case we are again dealing with the relation of the university to the outside world.

STUDENTS

The Class of 1873, the first to graduate from Kansas, consisted of three students. When we began our study in 1959, Kansas had 7004 undergraduates—2331 women and 4673 men. Of these, 1028 students were married.[3] It is, thus, a large school, though nowhere near as large as the campuses in Berkeley, Urbana, Columbus, and elsewhere.

Size itself has some implications for the conditions affecting academic

[2] Thorstein Veblen, *The Higher Learning in America* (New York: B. W. Heubsch, 1918).
[3] These figures were made available to us by the University of Kansas Statistical Service.

work. In a small school, faculty members may know a large proportion of the students personally.[4] If they do, they can base judgments about them on a variety of evidence. In a larger school, even a medium-sized one such as Kansas, this becomes impossible. While every faculty member may know some students well enough to make personal judgments about them, the sheer number of students reinforces the apparent need for a bureaucratically organized method of assessing students—a system of grades and credits.

Kansas recruits its students primarily, though by no means entirely, from the state of Kansas. It admits all graduates of accredited high schools in the state. But not all prospective college students in Kansas apply to the University. Those who go elsewhere to college probably consist of two types. Some students, mainly from the upper-middle class, may prefer to go away to school; they will go, insofar as they are able academically and financially, to the famous colleges and universities of the East Coast; a few may go to West Coast schools. We do not know how many of these there are, but they are thought of by the administration and faculty of Kansas as a loss; they are students the University would like to have if it could.

Other students know the University's reputation as the best, most academic, and most intellectual university in the area. Kansas is sometimes referred to as the "Harvard of the West." While those who make the statement understand the differences between Kansas and Harvard, they do not make it facetiously or ironically. It represents both an assertion of academic excellence and the intention to become even more excellent. Some students may feel that, because of its academic standards, they will not have the good time they believe necessary for a full college life if they go to Kansas. Others may simply fear that they will not be able to make the grade and will flunk out. (Both of these are possibilities. Kansas is much less of a "party school" than many others in the surrounding region. Similarly, many students do flunk out, because they are not able to meet its academic standards.) These students go to nearby state universities or to smaller local colleges and universities, in search of a better or easier time.

Not all students come from Kansas, however. Some come from out of state and some from foreign countries. Although they provide some geographical heterogeneity, the University still has, in general, the flavor of a Kansas institution. Its people are, in the main, Kansans (the second largest group comes from neighboring Missouri, particularly from the

[4] This, however, is only a possibility, not a necessity. Data from Amherst indicate that students see far less of faculty than might be expected in a small college. See Robert Birney et al., "The Class of 1959 at Amherst College," mimeographed, 1960.

contiguous Kansas City area) who are going to KU because they think they will get a good academic education there. The resulting student body is quite serious about academic work.

However, of the students who come to Kansas for this reason some are not as well equipped as others. Therefore, the University has the problem of creating a program for students who are well-motivated and well-prepared and at the same time dealing with a substantial number of students whose motivation may be good but whose preparation is not. As an increasing proportion of college-age youth goes to college, this problem can be expected to persist. Kansas will continue to get good students, but they will be mixed in with a number of those who are not so capable. That mixture sets certain problems for the University staff, as well as for the students and their organizations. Among other things, it provides the basis for easily made distinctions among students. Some students manage to deal adequately with the high standards of KU and others do not; students and others thus find it possible to make distinctions among students on the basis of how well they do academically.

LIVING GROUPS

Kansas is a residential college. Most of its students come from outside Lawrence and find housing in one of the several types of residential units available on or near the campus. College students use the term "living group" to refer to these units, and we adopt the usage here. The term refers both to individual houses and to the larger categories of similar types of housing (such as fraternities or dormitories); which of these we mean will be clear in context.

Living groups constitute the major form of stable institutionalized organization among students and thus play an important part in setting the conditions under which perspectives on academic work develop. By developing campus organizations (particularly living groups) from which the University benefits, students can and often do acquire (as we have already noted) a substantial amount of power and a fair measure of autonomy. Because living groups do have the opportunity for autonomy, they can, if they are able, organize for themselves the kinds of activities they will undertake in the area of academic work. Living groups thus become one of the major loci of the organization of collective student action with respect to academic work.

Furthermore, living groups typically contain members from each of the years in school, from freshman to senior. (The one exception is found in the sororities, which house no freshmen; the freshmen women's dormitory, on the other hand, does include counselors who are upperclassmen.) They thus provide the stage on which face-to-face interaction between new and older students most frequently takes place, the setting in which perspectives can be passed on from one class to the next.

Various aspects of living-group organization have an influence on the development of academic perspectives, and differences among the living groups affect the degree of emphasis placed on various aspects of a perspective. Variations in the ambitions, organization, and abilities of living groups and their members create variations in the kinds of activities that it is possible and reasonable to undertake.

Kinds of Living Groups

There are three major kinds of living groups at KU: fraternities and sororities (which we will refer to, for convenience and in acceptance of common usage, as "Greek" houses); organized independent houses; and unorganized independent groups. Table 2 shows the distribution of undergraduates among them.

TABLE 2
Distribution of Undergraduates by Sex and Living Group (Fall, 1959)

	Men	Women	Total
Fraternities and sororities	1593	744	2337
Scholarship halls	242	188	430
Residence halls (dormitories)	905	904	1809
Unorganized housing (apartments, rooming houses, commuters, married, and cooperatives)	1933	495	2428
Total	4673	2331	7004

Source: University of Kansas Statistical Service.

Kansas has a strong fraternity-sorority system. Forty-three Greek-letter organizations maintain houses on the campus. Of these, three are professional fraternities, which are also used, in some cases almost exclusively, by graduate students. Twenty-seven are men's social fraternities and thirteen are sororities. Local chapters often win prizes for being the best chapter of the year in their national organization, and individual students win recognition as the best member of their organization nationally. Such characteristic features of fraternity-sorority life as discriminatory recruitment and hazing have come under strong attack on many campuses, but the KU Greeks have forestalled such assaults by a variety of "progressive" actions. For example, they have turned the traditional Hell Week for pledges into an occasion for a mass cleanup of public highways and parks; they have organized pledge training programs along the principles of group dynamics; and they have placed strong emphasis on academic achievement among all their members (not just a few recruited "to keep the house average up").[5] The actions they have taken to maintain the system add to the already existing faculty pressure for academic performance.

Organized living groups of independents consist, like the Greek houses, of a number of students joined together in special housing set aside for students. Unlike the Greek organizations, they do not belong to any national organization, hence require fewer commitments from their members and have less control over whom they admit. The three major kinds of independent organized living groups are dormitories, scholarship halls, and cooperatives; the first two are university-owned.

The university maintains nine scholarship halls (five for men and four for women). Small buildings located near the campus, each houses about fifty students. Admission to these halls is usually granted as a scholarship to students with high scholastic standing who need financial assistance to attend the university. A student must maintain a high academic average to keep his place in such a house, just as he would have to do to keep any other scholarship award.

Before World War II, the university had few dormitories. After the war, however, it engaged in a large building program and had, in 1959, three residence halls for men and three for women, with more being built and planned. These residence halls, by far the largest residential units on campus, hold as many as 430 students and are organized like dormitories at other universities. The student pays fees in return for room and meals. Students living in residence halls are subject to university discipline, administered by a resident director appointed by the university, but do not have so complex and effective an internal organization as the Greek houses. There are also several cooperative living units on the campus. Students share the management of these houses and do all the work necessary to maintain them.

Students in the unorganized independent category may be of several types. In 1959, 1028 were married and lived either in apartments or rooms rented to them by private persons or in one of the housing projects for married students operated by the university. Unmarried students may live in rooms in private homes, may team up to share the cost of an apartment, or (if they are residents of Lawrence) may live at home with their parents. Most unmarried students living in private housing are men,

---

[5] Many Greek organizations on other campuses retain the practices more traditionally attributed to them in this area of activity. See Rose K. Goldsen et al., *What College Students Think* (Princeton, N.J.: Van Nostrand Co., 1960), pp. 60–80, for some observations on this point.

although a few upperclass and graduate women students also have such housing.

Living Groups, Prestige, and Campus Identity

Because living groups are the basic organized form of collective student action, the living group one belongs to acts as a source of identity for the individual student on campus. Who he is depends in some large measure on where he lives. When we asked students to identify another student for us, they frequently responded by telling us to which campus living unit he belonged. If students were concerned with their own campus reputations, then, they had cause to be concerned with the reputation of their living group. To the degree that living-group reputations depended on members' academic performance, a further pressure toward high academic performance came into existence.

But a living group can be a source of identity only if it has some kind of reputation on campus, and not all do. This was brought home to us in several striking ways. For instance, we asked several informants to rank fraternity houses for us. After making a kind of conventional complaint that this was not possible because all fraternities were alike, most could identify the fraternities that were well thought of and also those thought worst. We found, however, that they neglected to include a number of fraternities in their rankings unless we specifically asked about them. These groups had no reputation of any kind, being neither "good" nor "bad." Such an organization does not furnish much of an identity for its members.

Similarly, we found that students who lived in the new residence halls were eager to create a reputation, preferably good, but better bad than none at all, for their living group. They wanted other people on the campus to know that the dormitory existed and to attribute some special characteristics, whatever they might be, to its residents. Only if the living group itself had some kind of collective reputation could it mean anything for the identity of any particular member. Thus members of these living groups might seriously discuss whether they should take some action that would lead to the dormitory being put on social probation (a severe punishment limiting their right to have parties and other social events for a period of time) in order to get a reputation for wild parties.

If a living group managed to achieve a campus reputation for itself, its members could then worry about what kind of reputation it was. Living-group reputations were based on a variety of criteria and considerations, which students often combined into a rough overall measure of prestige. Although the prestige ratings of many living groups were indefinite, enough consensus existed (particularly about the top and bottom of the scale) for groups to orient themselves toward improving their position vis-à-vis other groups, maintaining a stable position satisfactory to them, or preventing slips in their standing. Thus the criteria that were used to assess living-group prestige were likely to become the object of concerted striving by living group members. Insofar as group academic achievement played a part in prestige ratings (as we shall see in Chapter 4 it did), the stage was set for a further emphasis on grades.

Living Group Organization

Living groups differ, by virtue of who they recruit and the way they are organized, in the degree to which they find it necessary to act together with respect to academic work and in the kinds of actions they find it possible to undertake. Organizational variations affect the level of effort of the members and the objects of that effort.

The Greek houses, because of their partial freedom from University control, have more responsibility for their own fate than dormitories or scholarship halls. Their members, for instance, share responsibility for the financial well-being of the house and their monthly bill is adjusted to house expenses. If the group loses members, each remaining member's share in the cost rises accordingly. Thus it is financially necessary for fraternities to recruit enough students to keep their houses full. In dormitories and scholarship halls, the responsibility for keeping the house full (and for making it attractive enough to students to accomplish that goal) is the University's.

The responsibility for recruitment brings with it the power to control who is recruited. Fraternities and sororities pick among those who wish to join them in a way not available to residents of University-run housing, and their ability to choose their own members creates the conditions under which certain elements of an academic perspective become salient. For example, as we will see, students who do not make grades sufficiently high to meet University or Inter-Fraternity Council standards may be ineligible for initiation, with consequences for the monthly house bill. So Greek organizations may use the likelihood of achieving academic eligibility as a means of selecting recruits, thus creating a condition to which would-be members must orient themselves.

Furthermore, because recruitment is selective and thus carries some sort of distinction, membership once gained tends to be prized. Members of Greek houses do not move in and out of their living group at the rate other students do, though some move into apartments in their last years in school. The intimacy and continuity created by a stable membership makes it relatively easier for Greeks than for independents to achieve collective action in academic work, as well as in other campus endeavors. Because they are more capable of sustained collective action than independent living groups, the Greek houses find it both easier to build a reputation for themselves and more imperative to mold that reputation as best they can, since they are more likely to be held collectively responsible for what their members do.

Finally, because recruitment is selective and members use house activities and offices as rewards more effectively than members of other living groups, Greek organizations find it far easier to exercise discipline over their members than do independent living groups. The ability to sanction nonconformity adds to their capacity for sustained collective action. They thus find it easier to demand desired kinds of academic performance and to create the conditions in which that performance becomes possible.

CONCLUSION

We suggested in Chapter 1 that the student perspective on academic work, arising in a relation of subjection to university administrators and faculty, would develop as an adjustment to and a reflection of that situation. Such a formula requires us to specify what the superordinate parties to that relation of subjection require of their subordinates, so that we may see what it is that students are adjusting to. In this chapter we have begun that job, discussing some of the environmental features of the University that lead its personnel to put a strong emphasis on academic achievement.

The University of Kansas, we have seen, is a typical residential college in a typical Midwest college town. But, because of its relations to other groups and organizations, it does not resemble the familiar stereotype of the "rah-rah" college those characteristics bring to mind. Quite the contrary. The kinds of faculty and students it has recruited and the kinds of obligations it has by virtue of its mandate from the state have led it to adopt a kind of organization that constrains students to put substantial effort into their academic work. In addition, the organization of student living groups, the importance of living-group reputations for the identities of individual students, and the importance of academic performance for those reputations increase the emphasis on academic achievement.

We turn now to a more detailed discussion of the concept of perspective and to a description of the perspective KU students characteristically adopt toward academic work. Having done this, we will give a more detailed picture of the constraints on student academic activity and the specific conditions they grapple with in forging their collective response to the academic side of college life. The detailed picture, which we defer till Chapter 4, will be seen solely from the student's point of view, in contrast to some of the environmental features described in this chapter. While important for the development of student perspectives, environmental features are not always visible to students, having their effect as they are mediated through the people and groups that impinge on students' daily lives.

CHAPTER 3

THE GRADE POINT
AVERAGE PERSPECTIVE

As students interact with one another, with teachers, and with other college officials, they develop ideas that, because they are held in common, create a universe of discourse, a common frame of reference in which communication may take place. Similarly, they develop, as they interact in a variety of institutional settings and specific situations, patterns of individual and collective activity. The activities grow out of the ideas, being their logical extensions in action. They also give weight and meaning to the ideas, by creating patterns of everyday experience that make the ideas seem reasonable and appropriate to the situations they are applied to; in this sense, the ideas grow out of the activities. We refer to the complex of ideas and activities, taken together, as a *student perspective*.[1]

We are concerned, in this book, with the perspective students develop on their academic work. How do they view academic work and achievement? What actions do they consider appropriate or expedient? What

[1] "Perspective" is a term we first used in analyzing materials gathered during a study of medical students. [See Howard S. Becker, Blanche Geer, Everett C. Hughes, and Anselm L. Strauss, *Boys in White: Student Culture in Medical School* (Chicago: University of Chicago Press, 1961)]. Materials gathered by participant observation contain both descriptions of people's actions and statements of the beliefs that go with those actions. We needed a term for these two classes of data that would not falsely separate them and borrowed the term "perspective" for the purpose. As we studied several medical student perspectives comparatively, we came to use the term conceptually as well, drawing on the earlier work of George Herbert Mead [*Mind, Self and Society* (Chicago: University of Chicago Press, 1934)] and Tamotsu Shibutani ["Reference Groups as Perspectives," *American Journal of Sociology*, 40 (May, 1955), pp. 562–569]. A complete account of this theoretical development is contained in Blanche Geer, "The Terminology of Participant Observation," (unpublished manuscript).

actions do they undertake, both as individuals and collectively? What reasons do they give, to themselves and others, for what they do in this area of campus life?

COMPONENTS OF PERSPECTIVES

We can divide perspectives, analytically, into several components. They contain, first, *a definition of the situation,* a set of ideas describing the character of the situation in which action must be taken. Students share an understanding of what their world is like, what it allows them to do, what it insists that they do, and an understanding as well of why they are in that situation and what they can reasonably expect to get out of it. They define some features of their situation as of the utmost importance, see others as relatively neutral, and may be quite unaware of still others, in effect defining them as nonexistent even though they may affect their lives profoundly. (As an example of the latter, suppose that the University insisted that professors publish frequently; students might find it difficult to see professors outside of class but be unaware of the pressure that produced that result.)

The most important features in students' definition of the situation are the following: a statement of the goals one can reasonably strive for in the situation; a description of the organizations within which action occurs and the demands they make on participants; the rules, both formal and informal, by which one's action is constrained; and the rewards and punishments one may look forward to as a consequence of his performance.

One aspect of the definition of the situation deserves special mention. The various areas of college life are not separated in the everyday experience of the student, even though we separate them analytically in our discussion. The world of student organizations (both living groups and campus organizations) and the world of dating, friendship, and personal relations affect and are affected by what happens in the world of academic work. The student's definition of the situation takes cognizance of these reciprocal relationships among areas of college life. For our present purpose, the important thing is that students include in their definition of the situation the possible effect of their academic performance on their achievements in student organizations and personal relations and, likewise, the effect of these on their academic success.

Perspectives also contain a specification of the kinds of *activities* one may properly and sensibly engage in. Given the world as they have defined it, certain actions seem to students, if not always to others, to be "sensible," to be more or less realistic ways of dealing with the problems they see the environment posing for them. We can distinguish several kinds of action. Students take some actions to gather information about the character of the environment; for example, a person might attempt to discover what the expectations of others are that he must take into account in organizing his future activities. They take some actions to gather information about themselves, to find out how well they are meeting the demands of others, how they are regarded by others, and what punishments or rewards they can expect. They take still other actions in an effort to do what they see as necessary in order to meet the expectations of others successfully, both the expectations embodied in institutional requirements and those presented to them less formally.

Perspectives contain *criteria of judgment*, standards of value against which people may be judged. Since the definition of the situation contains a statement of the rewards available in the academic area, students, when they have occasion to discriminate among members of a status category, can use the distribution of those rewards as a criterion of judgment. They judge those who distribute the rewards—their teachers—on the basis of how the teacher's performance affects their own chances of satisfactory achievement. They judge themselves and other students on the basis of the quality of the institutionally available rewards received.

The several aspects of the perspective form, in the everyday commonsense world of the student, a coherent whole. The perspective is not an explanation of student activity; it is a description of what students do and think and can be conceived as an explanation only in the sense that it constitutes the larger whole in relation to which any given student action or idea makes sense.

GENERALIZED GOALS

We have already said that perspectives are modes of collective action groups develop under the conditions set by the situations in which they have to act. The thrust of our analysis is largely situational, emphasizing the constraints and opportunities of the situation and minimizing the influence of ideas and perspectives that students bring with them to college. Yet students do bring with them some notions about college and what they are going to do there, and these have bearing on what actually happens, even though they are transformed in the student's later experience.

Students have, in a rudimentary way when they enter college and in more elaborated form afterward, a *generalized goal,*[2] a point of view

2 The concept of generalized goal is related to, but not the same as, the concept of long-range perspective used in Howard S. Becker, Blanche Geer, Everett C. Hughes, and Anselm L. Strauss, *Boys in White, op. cit.,* pp. 35–36, 68–79. They are alike in pointing to very general definitions of the meaning of one's participation in an organi-

about why they have come to college and what they may reasonably expect to get out of their stay there. Generalized goals are, when the student first enters, a mixture of vague generalities and fragmentary specific desires, between which the student dimly apprehends some kind of connection. As he goes through school, he will probably (though not necessarily) come to a more precise definition of the general goal and will discern more complicated and precise relations between it and the specific goals he develops in particular areas of college life. The generalized goal can be seen in its full development in some of the thoughtful philosophical statements made to us by graduating seniors reflecting on the meaning of their college experience.

The chief characteristic of students' generalized goal, in its fully developed form, is an emphasis on college as a place in which one grows up and achieves the status of a mature adult. To manage one's college life properly (whatever meaning is attributed to that vague statement) shows that one has what it takes to be a mature adult, for the problems of college life are seen as much more like those of the adult world than anything that has come before. To do well in college, one must have the qualities students attribute to adults: the ability to manage time and effort efficiently and wisely, to meet responsibilities to other people and to the organizations one belongs to, and to cope successfully with the work one is assigned.

Probably few students achieve so coherent a statement of their generalized goal. Most, while they might assent to such a statement were it presented to them, never become that self-conscious. So, in some respects, our statement of students' generalized goals consists of the inferences we make from their more fragmentary statements and actions. In particular, incoming freshmen have not formulated a generalized goal so clearly. Such hints of it as we have are contained in their statements about why they chose to come to Kansas rather than some other college. Table 3 classifies the comments on this topic made by students who came to the campus during the summer for Previews (a kind of preschool Orientation Week). It shows that they were more likely to explain

zation. They differ in that long-range perspective refers the meaning to some state of affairs that lies beyond the end of the period of participation, while generalized goal refers the meaning to changes that take place during participation.

For further discussion of the relation between the understandings people bring with them to a situation and those they acquire in it, see Howard S. Becker and Blanche Geer, "Latent Culture: A Note on the Theory of Latent Social Roles," *Administrative Science Quarterly*, 5 (September, 1960), pp. 304–313. The question has been pursued in studies of prison culture; see, especially, John Irwin and Donald R. Cressey, "Thieves, Convicts and the Inmate Culture," *Social Problems*, 10 (Fall, 1962), pp. 142–155, and David A. Ward and Gene G. Kassebaum, *Women's Prison: Sex and Social Structure* (Chicago: Aldine Publishing Co., 1965), pp. 56–79.

their choice on academic grounds than on any other. Many students who used the academic criterion said that KU was the best place academically in the state or the region, or that it was better than other colleges they had considered. Others defined KU as best in a given field of study or said that it had been recommended to them as academically outstanding by high school teachers, counselors, or professionals in the field they hoped to enter. The following comment is typical:

> [I asked him if he had considered going anywhere out of state or to any other college in Kansas.] Well, I didn't think of going out of state because of the money but I did think about going to [a small college] for a while, but this is a better place. This has a very fine reputation academically so I decided to come here. [Do you think that the reputation that KU has with people is that it's good academically?] Yes, I think everyone thinks of KU as the best in the state academically. I am very pleased and excited to be here.
>
> *Male previewer, small town*

It is clear that a student who defines his college this way has decided to put himself up against a serious academic opponent; he intends to take the academic side of college seriously.[3]

One implication of students' emphasis on maturity, which becomes increasingly important as they participate more fully in college life and become more aware of the relevance of organizational and personal relationships, is that it raises the question whether a mature person will devote all his time and effort to just one of the several major aspects of college life. The faculty may think that academic work is all that is really important, just as an employer might perhaps feel that his employees should think of nothing beyond their work. But employees usually feel that they have other responsibilities and obligations, both to themselves and to others, and students too may decide that they must reject the faculty's one-sided emphasis in favor of a more mature balancing of the worth of the several valuable things to be gained out of the college experience. Maturity can thus come to have the meaning that one must accept the importance of academic work and achievement without going so far as to ignore other areas of effort which the faculty do not see as worthwhile.

The generalized goal students have on entering, then, may be no more than an idea that they are going to take their academic work seriously,

---

[3] It is worth noting that we began our fieldwork expecting to find quite the opposite—that students were as frivolous and "collegiate" as the worst stereotypes would lead one to believe. Though we took pains to look for evidence of that frivolity, our field experience led us to our present conclusion. See Blanche Geer, "First Days in the Field", in Phillip E. Hammond, ed., *Sociologists at Work* (New York: Basic Books, 1964), pp. 322–344.

work hard, and do well. That goal, broadened and its connections to other areas of college life made specific, exerts an influence on the perspective students develop on their academic work. It does not tell the student how to act while he is in college; it only points the direction in which an answer must be sought and specifies a criterion against which any solution to the problems of college life will have to be measured. The generalized goal does not tell students the precise perspective they

TABLE 3
Previewers' Reasons for Choosing KU

Criterion	Number of comments	Per cent of students making one or more comments (Base 57)
Academic excellence	54	74
Social development	25	39
Low cost	17	28
Relatives or friends	12	19
Miscellaneous	9	14
Total	117	

should adopt toward their academic work; many perspectives might satisfy its requirements. But the generalized goal does stand ready to tell students when a potential perspective is not in keeping with their long-range aims.

THE GRADE POINT AVERAGE PERSPECTIVE

The student's generalized goal enjoins him to be serious about college: to recognize it as a serious place where important things happen and to try to do well in all areas of college life as a sign of having achieved maturity. His perspective on academic work develops as he interacts with other students in an environment in which, as we shall see, grades are the chief form of institutionalized value and the institutional basis of punishment and reward in academic pursuits.

The perspective students develop on their academic work—we can call it the *grade point average perspective* [4]—reflects the environmental emphasis on grades. It describes the situation in which students see themselves working, the rewards they should expect from their academic work, the appropriate actions to take in various circumstances, the criteria by which people should be judged, and relevant conflicts in goals.

[4] We occasionally shorten this, in what follows, and refer to the GPA perspective.

In general, the perspective specifies the grade point average as the criterion of academic success and directs students to undertake those actions that will earn "good" or adequate grades.[5]

The main elements of the grade point average perspective are these:

Definition of the situation

1. The college is so organized that one can neither remain as a student nor graduate without receiving adequate grades. Furthermore, a number of other rewards that students desire cannot be achieved without sufficiently high grades.

2. A successful student, one who is achieving maturity in college, will "do well" in his academic work, however "doing well" is measured, thus demonstrating that he is capable of meeting the demands of the environment and also opening the way to to success in other areas of campus life.

3. Doing well in academic work can be measured by the formal institutional rewards one wins. Since the major academic rewards are grades, success consists of getting a "good" grade point average.

4. Intellectual or other interests may suggest other rewards than grades to be sought in academic experience. Where the actions necessitated by the pursuit of grades conflict with other interests, the latter must be sacrificed.

Actions

5. To be successful a student should do whatever is necessary to get "good" grades, not expending effort on any other goal in the academic area until that has been achieved.

Criteria of judgment

6. Since any student who wants to can achieve adequate grades, failure to do so is a sign of immaturity. Grades can, therefore, be used as a basis of judging the personal worth of other students and of oneself.

7. Faculty members may be judged, among other ways, according to how difficult they make it to achieve adequate or "good" grades.

[5] We will use the expression "good grades" to refer to the level of grades that a student finds satisfactory, given the standards that he, his living group, and his other associates have developed. Those standards will take into account the various other obligations and opportunities relevant to the achievement of a mature balancing of effort and activity. "Good grades" will thus vary among students, living groups, and possibly along other dimensions as well. In contrast, we will use the expression "adequate grades" when we wish to refer to grades that are sufficient to meet some formal requirement; unless otherwise specified, "adequate grades" will refer to the GPA necessary to remain in school. Adequate grades, of course, do not vary, except as the requirement to which they refer varies.

To say that student perspectives emphasize grades does not mean that there is a unitary standard for all students. What is considered "good" may vary considerably among various groups on the campus. An average of B may be considered adequate in one fraternity house but substandard in another. The grade point average that will satisfy an engineering student may not satisfy a business student or vice versa. The definition of "good" grades depends, as well, on the student's aspirations in other spheres of campus life. Failing grades are satisfactory to no one, but any other set of grades may be acceptable to some student. Although the acceptable level of grades varies from group to group and person to person, the perspective directs students to orient their activities toward getting "good" grades.

An analogy with a money economy, which we later develop further, is instructive. Anyone participating in such an economy will want to make what might variously be described as "enough money," "good money," or "a decent living." But the conception of "enough" or "decent" will vary widely among social classes, occupations, regions—and between individuals as well. Some will be satisfied only if they are millionaires; some will settle for a bare subsistence; most are in between. Almost everyone recognizes that "money isn't everything," that one must balance the need for money against other needs which are equally important.

Similarly, students vary in the degree to which they personally accept and live according to the rules suggested by the perspective. To some it seems completely normal: "How else could things be?" Others recognize that things might, in some other institutional setting, be quite different, but find the perspective acceptable. And some are irked by it, find it constraining and uncongenial. But it has two features that cause most students to accept it, however they feel about it, as a reasonable way to view the campus world and act in it. First, it is a realistic way to orient oneself toward the academic aspects of campus life. To be sure, it may not be the only realistic orientation; but it takes account of what are objectively discernible features of the campus environment. For this reason, it works; a student who adopts it as a standard of action will probably not have academic troubles. Thus, even though other perspectives might produce equally acceptable results, students will probably use this one, because it has worked in the past.

Second, the grade point average perspective is widely accepted and thus has the force of being "what everyone knows." Most people the students come in contact with talk and act in ways congruent with it; it embodies the accepted commonsense of his world. To question it or act in ways that deny it requires the student to violate the commonsense assumptions his fellows share; it is easier and more natural to accept them.

Whatever the student's private reservations—and, indeed, no matter how many students may have such private reservations—the terms and assumptions of conventional discourse are those contained in the perspective. To recur to the analogy with money, an adult may feel that money is not very important and privately decide that he will ignore it; but as long as he lives in a money economy, surrounded by people and institutions that assume the importance of money, he will be constrained to accept that assumption in his dealings with them. Just so with students and grades; however the student feels privately, campus life is organized around the terms and assumptions of the grade point average perspective.

INTERACTION, CONSENSUS, AND PERSPECTIVES

Perspectives grow and persist in the course of students' interaction with one another and with college functionaries. They are not individual responses to the problems of college life but collective ones—collective in the sense that the understandings contained in the perspective are held in common and the actions contained in it are intelligible within that framework of understanding. They are collective, too, in being embodied in interaction, as students teach, learn, and transmit them in the course of the routine activities of college life.

In discussing the development of academic perspectives among medical students we were able to show that they interacted with respect to the same set of academic problems and arrived at consensus.[6] It is not possible to show interaction and consensus so directly in the case of the college. Though students' problems are essentially similar, they vary (and students' conceptions of them likewise vary) depending on differences in ability, living group, and in the specific kind of classroom imperatives students are subject to. In addition, it is clearly impossible for several thousand college students to engage in the kind of face-to-face interaction carried on by the much smaller medical student group. The resulting perspective is necessarily more general than it would be if students saw their problems as more nearly the same and if student interaction were more extensive.

The most pervasive aspects of the perspective relate to those aspects of the college that present the most similar kinds of problems to students. All students must meet certain minimum academic requirements if they are to remain in the college; the problems associated with these requirements are the focus of the most commonly held understandings. Even

---

[6] See the discussion of interaction, consensus, and perspectives in Becker et al., *op. cit.*, pp. 135–157.

here there is likely to be variation associated with differences in living group, classroom experience, and individual ability.

Other aspects of the perspective are related to the interconnections between various subgroups in the college. Though their perceived problems differ, students from different living groups, for instance, nevertheless find it necessary to interact in many different situations: the classroom, where they face the demands of a particular teacher; in student organizations, where they must cooperate in problems of administration, recruitment of personnel, and the like; and in heterosexual social life. The connections of these with one another and with the academic requirements of the college make necessary a common language and frame of reference within which interaction may proceed, and some aspects of the GPA perspective provide this framework.

The perspective thus exists as a more or less codified set of ideas and conventional practices, sometimes very explicit, sometimes almost totally implicit. Students may deduce the proper course of action from its ideas when they are in the company of other students; or they may adopt practices suggested to them by others and later find the justification in the perspective. Students, interacting with one another in a variety of ways and settings, maintain those elements of the student perspective on academic work passed on to them by older students, in the form of traditional precept and organizational practice, and develop new ones as new problems come up, even though we cannot demonstrate the presence of interaction and the development of consensus in every case.

Some students, thoughtful analysts of the circumstances of their own lives, can state student perspectives in a general and theoretical way. Others, less thoughtful or less articulate, simply state or act on the practical conclusions to be drawn from such an analysis, but their actions and statement imply the more generalized statement. The failure of some to express a perspective in general terms does not mean that it does not inform what they think and do, and we have not hesitated to attribute perspectives to less articulate students, on the basis of statements or actions congruent with the perspective.

The picture one should have, then, is of students going about their daily activities, arriving at joint definitions of situations and problems, working out solutions in the light of their common understanding of the situation, and engaged in what seem to them to be appropriate actions [7]—all of this informed by and carried on in the context of the body of collectively held ideas and collectively enacted patterns of activity that we have called a perspective.

[7] *Cf.* David Matza, *Delinquency and Drift* (New York: John Wiley and Sons, 1964), p. 132.

INFLUENCES ON THE DEVELOPMENT OF PERSPECTIVES

Several elements of social structure and individual student characteristics provide the context within which student perspectives on academic work develop. These elements influence the content of the GPA perspective, in ways we merely suggest here and elaborate at appropriate points in our analysis.

Students find that they must carry on their serious attack on academic work in an *environment of organizations* and organizational rules and practices, an environment that presents obstacles and poses problems. The attempt to be serious takes on more specific meaning and is transformed into an effort to do what the college requires and thus demonstrate that one is capable of dealing in an adult way with the responsibilities of a student.

The organizational environment furnishes the realities out of which students construct their definition of the situation. Students do not automatically respond to every feature of the environment. Some organizational realities, however, are very likely to be included in students' definition of the situation. When, for instance, an organizational rule is relatively strictly applied to all students, so that anyone may suffer by failing to meet its requirements, and when substantial numbers of students suffer in this way, it is unlikely that student perspectives will ignore that feature of the environment. On the other hand, a rule that affects few people and is seldom enforced will be an unlikely candidate for inclusion in the definition of the situation.

The college's administration and faculty have created an important part of the organizational environment: a curriculum, a set of courses and customary ways of running them, and criteria of academic achievement. The actions of the college administration and faculty provide the single most important environmental context within which students attempt to achieve their specific and general goals.

But other organizations also set conditions within which students construct their academic perspective. Student organizations, both living groups and campus organizations, also have rules to which students must accommodate themselves. In some areas student groups have no formal organization as such and no codified body of rules, but do have customary practices that exert an influence on students' academic work.

The organizational context supplies specific criteria students can incorporate into their definition of the situation, thus giving some concrete specification to their generalized goals. Organizational criteria may thus shape students' notions of what they are to strive for in the area of academic work. The organizational context also sets the conditions under which students strive for what they want. The rules of the college and of the various student groups set limits to the kind of behavior students can successfully engage in and the kind of means they can use toward their ends; their definition of the situation is likely to take cognizance of these constraints.

More detailed constraints arise in the *immediate environment* of the classroom where each teacher states more or less exactly what is required of the student in his class. Teachers vary, so that a student may be confronted with several different sets of demands in the course of his academic week. Each student, typically, deals with different faculty members and, consequently, widely held student perspectives must be quite general. Variations in the faculty one confronts in class contribute to variants of the general perspective, as do the next two elements we consider: the student's ability and the living group to which he belongs.

Students and faculty view the relation between academic achievement and the *individual ability* of the student differently. The student, from a common faculty point of view, does as well in his academic work as his abilities and motivation allow him to do; if he does poorly, it is because he cannot or will not do better. Those who think individual ability and motivation are the chief variables affecting student performance may have in mind either innate traits or traits acquired through earlier training. In either case, they conceive of motivation and ability as variables which it is the faculty's job to maximize.

Students do not share this view. They think that the student controls his own academic fate by the amount of effort he puts forth. They believe any student can do well in his academic work if he wants to. They do not believe that any student who has reached the point of entrance to the college is so deficient in ability or motivation as to be unable to perform adequately. They thus attribute variations in student performance to an unwillingness to give sufficient time and effort to academic work or to a deliberate decision to put one's major effort elsewhere.[8]

In our analysis, we are less concerned with the causes of variation in achievement (though in general we tend to agree more with students than with faculty) than we are with its effects on student perspectives. As we went about our fieldwork, we noted that some students seemed "bright" and others seemed "slow"; we made this informal judgment on the basis of the difficulty students reported in doing schoolwork, their

[8] This view, of course, can only be held when students' experience tends to confirm it, that is, when the work is such that it conceivably could be done at an adequate level if one were to work very hard. Such conceptions cannot be maintained when, as in the medical school we studied, the work is defined as impossible to complete and students' experience confirms the definition. See Becker et al., *op. cit.*, pp. 107–134.

grades and the apparent reasons for their grade level, and our own observation of their study habits and the ease with which they grasped
their academic work. For whatever reasons the difference occurred, it
clearly affected the kind of difficulty students had in meeting the requirements of their classwork, of the college, and of other relevant organizations and thus influenced the development of the GPA perspective.

Living groups provide one of the major settings in which student perspectives on academic work take on specific form. Every student, as we
have seen, belongs to some living group: an organized house, such as a
fraternity or sorority, a scholarship hall, or a dormitory. He may be a
hometown boy and live with his parents. He may live in a rooming
house. He may be married and set up in housekeeping. Although "living
group" conjures up an image of a highly organized group, we may by
extension regard any residential situation as characteristic of some group
or another, whatever its degree of organization.[9]

The demands of the college are mediated by and transformed in the
living group. As the student acts to meet the demands of college and
classroom as he has defined them, he finds that they take on a specialized
character because of the way they mesh with the obligations he has to
his living group. (Some living groups impose minimal obligations on
their members, but these may be thought of simply as the extreme case.)
In addition, the conditions of daily life characteristic of a living group
affect the student's ability to meet his classroom responsibilities. Differences in living groups are thus likely to produce characteristic variations
in the GPA perspective.

Living groups themselves respond to the situation in which they see
themselves vis-à-vis other organizations on campus. A salient aspect of
the living group's situation, as we have seen earlier, is its position in the
prestige hierarchy of campus living groups. Living groups tend to judge
actions and events and to organize their activities as their concern for
their own prestige dictates.

The elements we have considered, taken together, constitute the major
influences on the development of the GPA perspective. Students with a
given generalized goal, in the context of their definition of the organiza-

---

[9] We did not find that friendship groups based on year in school, major, occupational
goals, or similar matters played any important role in the development of the GPA
perspective. The influence of such groups is thought by many to be substantial; indeed,
we ourselves expected to find such influence, but our data refused to bear out that
expectation. See, for other views, Theodore M. Newcomb and Everett K. Wilson, eds.,
College Peer Groups (Chicago: Aldine Publishing Co., 1966), especially the essay by
Burton R. Clark and Martin Trow, "The Organizational Context," pp. 17–70. On the
other hand, Wallace's research tends to bear out the importance of residential groups
[Walter L. Wallace, *Student Culture* (Chicago: Aldine Publishing Co., 1966)].

tional imperatives of the college and of student organizations, enter the classroom where they learn the specific demands of particular faculty members. In attempting to meet those demands, they find their job made more or less difficult by their own individual ability. The demands of the college are mediated and transformed by their membership in a living group. Together, these conditions constitute the context within which students collectively construct the characteristic GPA perspective.

CONCLUSION

Because the several points of the perspective seem, both to students and to us, to form a coherent and understandable unity, we can think of the perspective as furnishing the underlying basis for many diverse and seemingly unrelated items of student thought and behavior. For this reason, we regard evidence about any one aspect of the perspective as evidence for the existence of the perspective in its entirety. Thus evidence that students seek to discover the requirements for getting a good grade is combined with evidence that they use grades to assess the worth of others and a variety of other kinds of evidence when we argue that the grade point average perspective is indeed the perspective generally used by students on their academic work.

We searched our field notes for all instances of behavior or conversation that gave evidence that students accepted and lived by the GPA perspective, that their thoughts and actions could be accounted for by supposing that they had adopted this perspective. At the same time, we looked for those items in our field notes that indicated that students did not accept the perspective, that their actions and thoughts reflected other perspectives instead. We begin by describing the various kinds of data that constituted positive evidence that students' thoughts and actions were congruent with the perspective sketched above. Every item that is counted in the tables presented in Chapter 9 has one or more of the characteristics we describe. In describing the kinds of evidence we have we will at the same time be giving a detailed account of the workings of the grade point average perspective, of the kinds of everyday interaction and conversation that embody it.

In the chapters that follow we first consider the students' definition of the situation in which they meet the problems of academic work: the larger organizational environment and the classroom. We next take up actions devoted to acquiring knowledge and information, watching students seek the information that will let them know what is necessary in order to achieve an adequate grade point average. We then turn to actions and find that students, both individually and collectively, organize their effort so as to achieve an adequate grade point average. We consider the bases on which students make judgments of other people, see-ing how these are affected by and reflect the influence of the grade point average. We end by giving certain summary measures of the evidence presented in our analysis. We use the measures to indicate the reasons for our belief that the GPA perspective exists and constitutes the con-trolling influence on students' academic behavior. We also consider the negative instances in our data, those observations that might be con-strued as evidence that the GPA perspective is not the students' major way of approaching the academic area of their college lives.

CHAPTER 4

DEFINITION OF THE SITUATION: ORGANIZATIONAL RULES AND THE IMPORTANCE OF GRADES

The rules and procedures imposed by college faculty and administration create a framework within which individual students and student groups organize their academic activities. The rules and procedures, both official and unofficial, of student groups similarly create a set of conditions to which students must adjust.

Although the frameworks of action so created have an objective existence and affect the *lives* of students whether students are aware of it or not, they affect student *perspectives* only insofar as they are incorporated into students' definition of the situation. Rules and procedures vary in their influence on student perspectives. Those governing the continuation of participation in the college are likely to be part of the perspective of those who remain in school; if they were not, students might easily run afoul of them and be forced to leave. Rules and procedures that affect many areas of a student's life will be more likely to affect perspectives than rules whose effects are confined to one area, and rules that are regularly enforced are more likely to be defined as a relevant part of the situation than those that are not.

In the academic area students stand in a relation of subjection to the faculty and administration, who make rules and devise procedures unilaterally. The rules of American colleges, though they vary in detail from school to school, are remarkably similar (except, perhaps, for a few rare experimental schools). The college provides a four-year program, during which students take a combination of required and elective courses in a variety of fields. Faculty committees devise programs of instruction indicating which students are to take what courses in what sequence. The faculty use assignments and examinations to discover how well the student has learned what he is supposed to, and award grades on the basis of performance. The student's grades determine whether he remains in school and what further courses of action are open to him.

The rules of the college governing academic work may be found in its catalog and in other official documents. They ordinarily apply uniformly to all students, although in some cases they may vary for different categories of student (as, for instance, when there are somewhat different rules for upperclassmen). But college rules seldom touch students directly. Rather, they gain specificity and meaning, and have more potential for affecting student action, as their importance is defined for the student in the smaller social structures in which he has his everyday experience.

The definition of college rules as important in campus social structures has several important features. First, the rules take on a great deal of variety as they are mediated by specific teaching situations. Courses vary in the way they are set up. Although every course requires the student to do some work to perform successfully, the definitions of appropriate work and level of effort can vary considerably, as can the number and kind of faculty and subfaculty personnel with whom the student must deal. Students take account of this variation in their definition of the situation.

Second, the impact of college rules is mediated by the organizations students belong to, both living groups and campus organizations. These groups interpret college rules to their members, sometimes denigrating and sometimes exaggerating their importance. They make use of the framework of college rules, in part, in organizing and running their own affairs. And their own activities are (as they are well aware) governed by other rules that make use of the rules about academic work.

Third, and a consequence of what has just been said, the actual impact of university rules about academic work on the student and on his definition of the situation will vary according to the classes he takes and the living group and other student organizations he participates in. The standards set by the rules will be easier to satisfy in some classes than in others. The impact of failing to satisfy them, or of satisfying them minimally, will be defined differently by students who belong to different living groups or who are involved in different campus organizations.

Taken together, the social organization and system of activity defined by college rules, as they are mediated through classrooms and student groups, constitute the conditions under which the student builds his definition of the situation in which he pursues his academic work. The chief characteristic of this definition is that it makes the grades awarded by the faculty the major institutionalized reward available for academic work.

UNIVERSITY RULES ABOUT GRADES

In describing the students' definition of the situation in which they do their academic work, we are somewhat hampered by the degree to which they habitually take these matters for granted. For instance, students do not ordinarily talk to one another about the grading system. They know, and assume that everyone else knows, that grades are given, that they vary from A to F, that college work is organized in courses, that one must have a major to graduate, and many similar matters. When they do speak of such things, they refer only to their effects; thus students did not describe the grading system to us, but they did speak of having difficulty "making their grades" and of the undesirable consequences of failing to make them.

For this reason, we have relied in this chapter heavily, but not exclusively, on official documents of the college and other campus organizations, in which the rules students define as important aspects of the situation are stated. We do not, however, cite rules at random or indiscriminately. Rather, we cite those rules whose importance students made plain to us by taking cognizance of them in organizing their own activities. This chapter, then, contains a student's-eye view of the rules, procedures, and customs relevant to academic work. In a number of cases, we follow the rule with an example of the kind of student statement or action that brought it to our attention as a relevant part of the student's environment.

The campus-wide rules made by faculty and administration specify when grades are to be given, in what form they are to be given (i.e., as letter grades or numerical grades), and the actions to be taken toward students whose grades fail to meet minimum requirements. Most importantly, the rules determine the circumstances under which one may remain a student or be required to leave school. Students take account of these rules in defining their academic situation and their academic problems.

Individual course grades are less important than the combined grade point average (GPA). The GPA, calculated every semester and cumulatively over the time one has been in school as well, is part of the student's official record and furnishes the raw material for many published University statistics. It takes into account both the grade earned and the number of hours of credit for which one is taking a course. The student ordinarily receives one hour of credit for each hour the class meets a week (a class that has three hourly sessions a week gives three credit hours), although occasionally more credit will be given. To find the GPA for the semester one multiplies the number of credit hours for each course by three if the grade is A, by two if it is B, by one if it is C, by zero if it is D, and by minus one if it is F. The total of one's grade points is then divided by the number of credit hours taken. The resulting GPA varies from plus three to minus one; a student who receives all A's has an average of 3.0, a student who receives all F's has an average of —1.0, and so on. In some colleges different numerical values are assigned (an A might receive four points and an F none, for instance), but the method of calculation is generally the same.

A substantial number of students find grades a problem. Table 4

TABLE 4
Distribution of Grades, All Undergraduates
(Fall, 1961)

Grade point average	Number	Per cent
2.00 and above	1886	25
1.00–1.99	3234	43
0.99–0.81	352	5
0.80–0.01	1209	16
0.00 and below	852	11
Total	7533	100

Source: Registrar's Office.

shows the distribution of grades for all undergraduates in the fall semester of 1961. Only 25 per cent of the students received a GPA of 2.0 or better (a B average). At the other extreme, 32 per cent of the students received a GPA below 1.0 (a C average).

University regulations provide that students whose GPA in any semester is below zero will be dropped for poor scholarship. The Committee on Scholarship and Probation may, at its discretion, permit the student to enroll for another semester; nevertheless, a student whose GPA is zero or less is in imminent danger of being forced to leave. He can transfer to another school, but he cannot return to the University of Kansas without special permission.[1]

Freshmen and sophomores whose GPA is below .70 are put on probation, as are juniors and seniors whose GPA is below 1.00. A student on

[1] *Bulletin of the University of Kansas,* 59, No. 10 (October 1, 1958), p. 73.

probation who fails to achieve the required GPA in his next semester can also be dropped from school for poor scholarship and, at the least, must have the permission of the Committee on Scholarship and Probation to enroll for the next semester.[2] (The categories in our table do not, for technical reasons, quite match the categories used in the rules, since the table divides students at .80 while the rules make .70 the point at which students are put on probation. If this cutting point were used, 27 per cent of the enrolled undergraduates would be dropped from school for failing grades.)

The consequences of these rules are vividly apparent to students in danger of failing:

> In fact, if something doesn't happen about my grades pretty soon, I'm going to end up in boot camp by this time next year. [You mean you'll get drafted?] Either that or I'll enlist. I'll have to do something if I get those kinds of grades any more and flunk out. . . . I'd pretty well have to go into the army or something. My old man isn't going to be very happy just having me sit around the house.
>
> *March, 1960, independent sophomore*

Many students spoke of their fear of failing or said simply that they were having trouble with their grades. In such cases, the unspoken premise in their argument referred to the rules we have just cited.

The grade point average is calculated for the entire time one is in school, as well as for the current semester. This cumulative average affects those who manage to raise their previously lower grades to a C average, for they will not be able to graduate unless they make in future semesters a GPA sufficiently higher than a C average to offset their low grades in the past. Regulations for graduation from the College of Liberal Arts and Sciences specify that students must earn a total of 124 grade points to graduate and that they must earn a minimum of one grade point for every hour of credit in their major subject.[3] Thus the student's past sins remain to haunt him for semesters to come:

> I don't want to be in school forever. You see, you have to have an over-all C average to graduate, over-all your four years, and I'm not going to do it unless I pull up above a C on some of my grades, because my other grades are so lousy.
>
> *April, 1960, independent sophomore*

Students with better averages may also have cause for alarm. Students who have won scholarships may have to achieve quite a high average to

[2] *Ibid.* These rules applied to the College of Liberal Arts and Sciences; other Schools in the University had somewhat different standards.
[3] *Ibid.*, p. 63.

keep the scholarship for another year. Although the committees and administrators who oversee scholarship awards do not apply rules mechanically, they do in general follow certain guidelines in renewing awards. For some scholarships, an average as high as 2.5 may be desirable:

> . . . If you begin to get more B's than A's they begin to think about whether they should let you continue with the scholarship or not. He [the Dean] didn't explicitly say 2.5 but if you begin to get more B's than A's that would mean that you were beginning to drop below a 2.5.
>
> *July, 1960, fraternity senior*

Students who lose their scholarships may have to leave the university for financial reasons.

Even if the student remains on campus, his grades affect the kind of life he can lead. The regulations affecting extracurricular student organizations penalize students with low grades. A number of regulations specify a minimum grade point average as a condition for participation in campus activities. The most inclusive rule, passed by the University Senate and included in the "Eligibility Rules for Participation in Extracurricular Activities," states:

> Any undergraduate student of the University must meet the eligibility regulations set forth in paragraph three below in order to participate in extracurricular activities. All University-related organizations and activities not directly connected with the classroom come under the jurisdiction of this rule.[4]

The rule itself, given in the next paragraph, is tempered by not being applied to mere membership in organizations. Rather, "Students representing the organizations in intra-mural activities, or holding position of responsibility or leadership, such as officers, members of executive boards or working committees, must meet the requirement of eligibility." This is still a great many people, for a large number of students hold such offices at some point during their college careers. To be denied an office under the Senate regulation is a serious deprivation, even if one does not particularly desire office; it is an indignity, rather like being deprived of the right to vote, even though one has never exercised it.

To be eligible for office, the student must be taking at least twelve hours of classes. In addition, he must, in effect, have a C average:

> For those who have attended college one semester or more, at least sixty per cent of the grades in all college subjects attempted within the last calendar

---

[4] "Eligibility Rules for Participation in Extracurricular Activities," a mimeographed document of the University Senate, University of Kansas.

year immediately preceding the opening of the semester of participation in the activity must be C or better.[5]

A final rule states that anyone who has been in college a year or more must have completed at least twenty-four hours of work for credit during the year preceding. The Committee on Eligibility of the University Senate reserves the right to make exceptions to the rules when they might result in gross injustice.

The rules, no doubt, are not always enforced strictly, for University officials have discretionary powers of enforcement. But this does not mean that students will define the rules as flexible. They do not know, until the event, whether any given case will be decided according to a strict or flexible interpretation of the rules and therefore orient themselves to the rules as presented, rather than relying on the possibility that theirs will be the case in which an exception is made.

STUDENT ORGANIZATIONS

The student with low grades may incur a number of other disabilities, not because the faculty or administration make rules decreeing the disability, but because student groups make use of the GPA, both formally and informally, as a way of sorting people out for reward and preferment. Student organizations adopt formal rules tying membership and participation to grades. In addition, students use the GPA as an informal way of choosing among other students, both for organizational positions and in less structured situations. Because of the interconnections between student activities, the disabilities incurred in one area of campus life produce further disabilities in other areas, as we shall see later. Finally, the criteria by which students award prestige to living groups depend in part on the members' GPA's and in part on their achievements in other areas affected by the GPA. Since the prestige of one's living group is an important component of student identity, students suffer when their living group suffers.

The impact on the student varies with his actual membership in organizations or his aspirations to membership; the student who does not want to belong to a particular organization feels no loss if rules forbid him membership when his grades fall below a given minimum. Some living groups demand that their members participate in extracurricular activities, dating, and other areas of student life, as well as performing adequately academically, and the student who belongs to one of them and receives low grades will think it a greater disability than a student who does not belong to a living group making such demands on its members.

[5] *Ibid.*

The regulations governing membership in fraternities and sororities make use of the GPA as a criterion. They divide all students into those who are eligible for initiation and those who are not. The rule for men, contained in the constitution of the Inter-Fraternity Council, states:

> To be eligible for initiation, a man must have received at least twelve credit hours in the school in which he was enrolled and must have attained a minimum grade average of 1.00, including D's and F's, and must have obtained such average and such credit hours during the semester in which he was pledged.[6]

Women do not pledge a sorority until they have been in school a semester and are not initiated until the end of their first year in school. Sororities can, therefore, apply the GPA criterion even earlier in the process, allowing no girl to go through Rush who has not had at least a C average in the preceding semester, with no incomplete grades. This rule, made by the University of Kansas Panhellenic Association (the women's version of the Inter-Fraternity Council), is supplemented by one on initiation:

> A pledge may be initiated if she has completed at the University of Kansas, in the semester immediately preceding the initiation, a minimum of twelve hours and has a 1.00 grade average with no failures in either credit or non-credit courses.[7]

Many organizations informally demand higher GPA's than the formal rules require. A number of fraternities and sororities, for instance, privately require pledges to have a higher GPA than the IFC or Panhellenic minimum. These requirements are usually kept secret, but one hears of Greek-letter organizations that insist on a GPA of at least 1.3 before they will initiate a new member. Student gossip, particularly in the freshmen women's dormitories, may exaggerate the strictness of the informal requirements.

The most explicit statements on this point come, not surprisingly, from freshmen women, who still do not know wether they will be asked to join sororities; for most men, the question is settled before school begins. Women incorporate these rules into their definition of the situation:

> One thing is, they really have a way to make all the freshman girls study very hard. It's because we can't pledge sororities right away. So naturally you want to make a very good record so that the sororities will be interested in you. It always helps to have good grades. . . .
>
> *November, 1959, freshman woman*

[6] Constitution of the Inter-Fraternity Council of the University of Kansas (first adopted in February, 1921; revised April 20, 1959).
[7] University of Kansas Panhellenic Association Handbook, 1959.

The rules assume great importance for some students:

> "I feel insecure if I'm not accepted and here that means the Kappas or the Thetas or the Pi Phis. I just have to begin at the top. . . . [A friend] just got into the Pi Phis. All her friends are in there and she only had a 1.27 but they just took her in." The observer said, "What are you supposed to have to get into one of those [prestige] sororities?" She said, "Well, I think it's pretty standard that you have to have a 1.5. . . ."
>
> *March, 1961, freshman woman*

The rules furnish the basis on which these girls perceive problems arising for them as a result of their academic performance.

Living-group rules affect a student's fate even after he becomes a member. In some houses various perquisites and minor rewards go to those who have high grades. In others, group rules restrict access to offices in the living group on the basis of grades. We did not collect documents on this point from all organizations and living groups, but one residence hall had a set of rules that may be quite common. Its constitution required that representatives and other officials of floor and wing governments have at least an overall 1.00 grade average. In addition, to become president or vice-president of the hall, an overall GPA of 1.5 was required.[8]

Students are aware of the many interconnections between different areas of campus life and recognize that failure in one area will have consequences in other areas. Thus freshmen who belong to fraternities are more likely to participate in campus organizations and thus have experiences that will prepare them for higher campus offices. If low grades keep a student out of a fraternity, his chances of achieving office suffer. And holding office, students think, has consequences beyond the college years, when the reputation one has earned in campus activities affects the kinds of jobs one is offered or, possibly, one's career in local and state politics.

Likewise, though there are no formal GPA criteria governing dating, it is clearly affected by those we have already discussed. Fraternity and sorority members are commonly thought to be desirable dates, if for no other reason than their membership in prestigeful groups, and they tend to date one another to a greater-than-chance degree. A student whose grades prevent him from joining a fraternity or sorority knows that he will lose the advantage of easy access to desirable members of the opposite sex which membership is thought to provide.

Students also meet desirable potential dates in such activities as serving on a committee of student government or planning an all-campus

[8] Constitution (of Templin Hall), mimeographed, n.d.

dance or party. The student knows that if low grades prevent him from participating or holding office in an organization where he might meet desirable dates, his social life will be adversely affected. Insofar as participation in living-group activities is unaffected by grades, the student of course retains his dating opportunities; he can meet desirable dates by, for instance, working on a joint fraternity-sorority float for the Homecoming Parade. Nevertheless, even though there are no formal grade requirements, some students recognize that success in dating is related to one's GPA.

We have already noted that the living group is a significant part of the student's campus identity. What affects his living group affects him, and he may be as concerned about the one as the other. His grades, and those of his fellow members, have a substantial effect on the fate of the living group. What the student wants for his living group must be gained with grades, both his own and those of all living group members, condensed in a house average.

Briefly, living groups have two major desires whose achievement may be hindered by low grades. On the one hand, the group wishes to continue to exist. For some groups, of course, this is not a problem. University residence halls (including scholarship halls) will continue to exist whether their current members make adequate grades or not. The University will find others to take the place of those who fail. But a fraternity or cooperative knows that it may cease to exist if a sufficient number of its members are forced out of school by low grades, for the individual's monthly house bill will rise, the amount of money available for parties will fall, and this, in a vicious circle, will affect recruiting adversely.

TABLE 5
Grade Point Averages of Living Groups (Spring, 1960)

Living group	Number of groups	Average	Range
All women		1.60	
Women's scholarship halls	4	1.99	2.09–1.88
Sororities	13	1.72	1.97–1.41
Women's residence halls	6	1.35	1.64–1.20
All men		1.32	
Men's scholarship halls	5	1.74	1.84–1.64
Fraternities	29	1.37	1.99–0.62
Men's residence halls	5	1.07	1.40–0.76
All university		1.41	

Source: University Daily Kansan (Summer Session), July 1, 1960.

The second major desire, being more difficult to achieve, seems more important to students. We have already noted the existence of a prestige system among living groups. An analysis of our field notes reveals that the single most important criterion students use to assess living-group prestige is the house grade point average.

The house GPA is a simple arithmetic mean of the GPA's of all living-group members who are residents and, as Table 5 shows, a high group GPA is as rare as an individual one. In the spring of 1960 the all-University average was 1.41, but the average conceals a great diversity. One women's scholarship hall had the highest GPA on campus: 2.09. At the other extreme, one man's residence hall had an average of 0.76 and one fraternity had 0.62. A high house average is a scarce commodity and achieving it is problematic for the living group.

Table 6 presents an analysis of all those items in our field notes in which statements were made about the relative prestige of living groups, categorizing them according to the criterion used as the basis for the assignment of rank. Although participation in extracurricular activities and intramural sports and the ability to give good parties also rank high as bases of prestige, grades are clearly the single most important criterion.

TABLE 6
*Criteria Used to Judge Prestige of
Living Groups*

Criterion	Total	Per cent
Grades	67	38
House participation in campus activities	46	26
Intramural sports	21	12
Parties	20	11
"Sharpness"	11	6
"All-round"	4	2
Wealth	3	2
Miscellaneous	5	3
Total	177	100

Because living groups recognize the importance of individual and house averages, those that control their own recruitment (primarily the Greek houses) attempt to recruit the best academic prospects they can find. Fraternities have some difficulty because, since they ordinarily pledge incoming freshmen, they must rely on the student's high school average alone in making their assessment. But it is clear that a potential pledge's grades are an important component of his attractiveness to a house, as this comment by the president of a fraternity attempting to improve its prestige indicates:

> Our scholarship wasn't too good. It wasn't bad but it wasn't too good, so this year we set out to improve it. I don't mean that we tried to get all scholars in the house, but we did get a very good smart pledge class. We pledged twenty-six guys and eleven of them were in the top ten per cent of their high school class.
>
> *January, 1961, fraternity senior*

Less obviously, other achievements that contribute to house prestige are partly dependent on the members doing well academically. The second most frequent criterion used to rank living groups is whether members of the group have achieved high office in extracurricular activities, and the third is the group's record in intramural athletics. In the case of activities, we have already seen that inadequate grades can prevent a student from attaining high office; it likewise prevents his living group from receiving the increment to its prestige that it might have if he had received the proper grades and had been eligible for office.

Similarly, a group's ability to field an athletic team or engage in other campus activities will be hampered if its members flunk out in midyear or feel they cannot devote the necessary time to sports. For instance, a group may have its skit selected for performance in a traditional campus theatrical revue. Asked if his fraternity had ever submitted a script to be judged for this competition, one member answered:

> No, to tell the truth, we haven't got enough fellows who are doing well grade-wise. A thing like this takes an awful lot of work and an awful lot of time and it's something that couldn't really be done by us.
>
> *February, 1961, fraternity sophomore*

In short, as the campus is organized, the conditions for achieving continued existence and high prestige require that living groups have members who can get grades that are at least adequate. If some substantial number of members fail to get adequate grades, the group's prestige cannot be maintained at a level satisfactory to the membership; if enough members fail, the group's existence may be threatened. In this way, the living group mediates and transforms the requirements of the college. It attaches another set of sanctions to low grades. Not only do low grades affect the individual student; they also affect the living group he belongs to and that part of his campus identity involved in his living group. Naturally, members of some living groups are affected more than others; a living group that has no aspirations for campus prestige or that is not organized to be a source of identity or to be able to control its members' conduct will have little further effect on college requirements. But well-organized groups, desirous of maintaining or improving their prestige, will add further incentives to those furnished the student by college rules.

GRADES: THE CURRENCY OF THE CAMPUS

The material we have just presented indicates that grades are the chief institutionalized valuable of the college. Of the many valuable things students can acquire, grades are the only ones that are formalized in an officially administered system applying to all students. In this the grading system closely resembles the operation of a money economy, with grades themselves playing a role analogous to that of money or currency in the community. Let us examine the implications of these statements.

What is valuable to one may not be to another. But people living together in a society, sharing a common culture, come to agree on certain things—*valuables*—as having a common value for all of them. When a society has a money economy, its members share a conception of the value of money. Money, embodied in currency, is one of the society's valuables, and members of the society know it is valuable, whether they themselves desire it very much or hardly at all. When something is commonly defined as valuable and when formal rules define for a society its character and how it is to be used, we may speak of an institutionalized valuable.

Grades are the major institutionalized valuable of the college campus. The players in the drama of college life—students, faculty, administration, and parents—all define grades as valuable, even though they may disagree about their value relative to other things. Furthermore, formal and informal rules define how grades are to be gained and the consequences of having grades of one kind or another.

Like money in the larger society, one must have adequate grades if one is to acquire many of the good things of the campus community, such as positions of influence and honor for oneself and one's living group. Again, like money, adequate grades are scarce. If a teacher marks on a curve, as many do, students compete for a share in the limited quantity of adequate grades just as businessmen compete for their share of the consumer's dollar. As the institutionalized scarce valuable of the community, grades come to be a measure of personal worth, both to others and to one's self, just as money does in the larger society.

Grades, of course, are not the only thing people in the college community consider valuable in the area of academic work. Many students think scholarship and personal intellectual growth are valuable things to acquire in college. But only some students think so; others do not consider scholarship of great importance. Everyone, on the other hand, recognizes the importance of grades. In this sense, the definition of grades as valuable is common to all participants in campus life, while the definition of scholarship and intellectual growth as valuable is not held in common.

Grades are universally defined as important because they are institutionalized; scholarship need not be recognized as important by everyone because its status as a valuable is not ratified by a set of rules and embodied in the organization and daily routine of the college. In the same way, participants in our society may consider beauty or truth more important than money. But one can ignore beauty and truth in one's life because they are not institutionalized; no one can ignore money, no matter how unimportant he thinks it. Not to have money has consequences one must reckon with. To have grades of the wrong kind likewise has consequences one cannot ignore.

Nevertheless, just as economic achievement is not the only important thing in a man's life, so academic achievement is not the only important thing in a student's life. A certain minimum is essential in each case, because of the way the valuable is institutionalized, with other kinds of rewards contingent on reaching that minimum. But beyond the minimum, which represents the level necessary in order to have the privilege of choosing where to put one's remaining time and effort, choice becomes possible, and the person finds that he must balance the various rewards available against one another in making that choice. One may decide to sacrifice the higher grade that would come with more work in a course, choosing to devote that time instead to a political career or a girl friend.

It is at this point that both economic man and the grade-getting student achieve some measure of autonomy. To be sure, they are both captives of a system of performance and reward imposed on them by others; the student is still in a relation of subjection to faculty and administration. But, having achieved the minimum without which participation is impossible, they can then choose to go no farther, to pursue instead other valuables in other areas of life. They become, thus, men in a community, fully alive to all the possibilities available to them in that communal life. As we shall see, students make use of that autonomy, though not in the ways that faculty members often hope they will.

THE FACULTY VIEWPOINT: AN ALTERNATIVE DEFINITION

We have described the university social structure, as students define its effects in the area of academic work, as one that emphasizes grades,

grades being the chief and most important valuable. Because this is a matter on which students and faculty have widely differing viewpoints, and because we tend to give more weight to the student viewpoint than academicians commonly do, we want here to indicate what seems to us the typical faculty viewpoint and to criticize it for failing to give sufficient weight to the structural imperatives we have described.

We have no systematic data on faculty attitudes toward academic work and grading systems. But we think it fair to suppose that many, though not all, faculty members would agree with the following statement by an articulate defender of faculty values:

> An English professor "spanked" Greeks last night for creating what he called an atmosphere "where emphasis on scholarship exists for the sole purpose of getting a grade."
>
> In a panel discussion of what the Greek system means to the University of Kansas, Professor A_____ spoke out against competition for the highest grade point averages which exists between Greek houses.
>
> "You must reflect a scholarly attitude instead of an attitude which is merely based on obtaining good grades," Prof. A_____ said.
>
> "You stress emphasis on scholarship for the mere purpose of obtaining a good grade," he berated members of fraternities and sororities. . . .
>
> "I know that you must stress the grade point average of the house to erase the idea that fraternity life is all games—I guess we'll have to call it a necessary evil," he said.
>
> "Still," he added, "I've always thought the object of the Greek system was to develop leaders. In stressing the grade point so highly, you do disservice to your house."
>
> Prof. A_____ said he thought the moral duty of the student is to get an "A" and not to tell anyone.
>
> "The satisfaction of scholarship is a personal thing," he said.
>
> In his talk, the educator lashed out at competition in scholarship. He said that most successful men have become that way by merely doing what they wished to do.
>
> "There are some boys who play football to get the chance to beat Oklahoma and there are some who play because they love the game. Scholarship is like that," he said.
>
> "In my classes I don't feel that anyone is competing against anyone else. I base the grades on whether or not the student has learned the material," the professor said.
>
> He said that scholarship begins "when a person wants to get the grade for himself and not for the organization." [9]

Yet we may also suppose that the faculty attitude toward grades is more complex than this. Some faculty members, no doubt, believe that the grades they give accurately reflect the amount of knowledge the stu-

[9] *University Daily Kansan,* March 23, 1960.

dent has acquired and are perfectly content that students should work for grades; in doing so they will learn what they are supposed to know. Other faculty members despise grades and would like to do away with them and all the associated paraphernalia of grade point averages, cumulative averages, and the like. Still others feel great ambivalence. They find it necessary, whether out of inner conviction or because of bureaucratic rules, to give grades and try to do it in a serious and responsible way. But they do not believe that the grades they give adequately reflect student ability; there are always some students who do well on tests although their classroom performance casts doubt on their grasp of the material presented, and others who know the material but get poor grades, perhaps because of poor test-taking skill. The faculty want to reward true achievement rather than the cunning of the accomplished grade-getter.

Faculty in the last two categories probably feel that students should be concerned about grades, but not *that* concerned. In particular, they object to what they see as the student tendency to reduce everything to grades, to raise interminable questions about "what we are responsible for," about the grading system and the criteria that will be used in assigning grades, about the number of questions on the exam—all the common questions that seem to them at best extraneous to the true business of learning and at the worst a deliberate mockery of it.[10]

Faculty are usually at a loss to explain student interest in grades and see no rational basis for it. They may attribute it to misguided competitiveness or to other kinds of irrationality. They do not see its basis in the structure of campus life, do not understand that the student definition of the situation is largely based on the realities of college life.

Faculty members, in complaining about student concern with grades instead of scholarship, complain, we may argue, because they feel that student concern with "beating" the system of tests and assignments designed to test achievement interferes with the true assessment of student ability. Students have a different view. They take tests and grades at face value and see a connection between doing their academic work properly—in such a fashion as to get adequate grades—and the emphasis on maturity contained in their generalized goal. They believe that when they achieve a satisfactory GPA they have demonstrated their ability to do their work and meet their obligations to themselves, their living

[10] See the discussion of medical faculty views in Howard S. Becker, Blanche Geer, Everett C. Hughes, and Anselm L. Strauss, *Boys in White: Student Culture in Medical School* (Chicago: University of Chicago Press, 1961), pp. 110 and 132–134. Several essays in Nevitt Sanford, ed., *The American College* (New York: John Wiley and Sons, 1962), give evidence of the viewpoint of college faculty members.

group, and their college—in short, their ability to act as responsible adults.

THE CONFLICT BETWEEN GRADES AND LEARNING

Despite what we have just said, some students share the faculty viewpoint in part. They incorporate it into their definition of the situation as one horn of a dilemma they see the college as posing for them. They feel that the workaday world of academic requirements, which forms the basis of the GPA perspective, causes them to miss something they might otherwise get from their courses, that they must meet the requirements before they can attempt to "learn for themselves." Insofar as the dilemma reflects a persisting definition of grades as important, it does not indicate the existence of a different and alternative perspective.

We do not mean to imply that students feel the conflict most of the time or that most students do at one time or another; the implication is not necessary to our argument, which is only that where the conflict is felt it reflects the belief that grades are important. For the most part, indeed, students believe that their courses are "good"; what they are required to do to pass the course is just what they ought to do anyhow to learn the substance of that course. Even when they fail to become excited by the content they are learning, they reason that the teacher knows the subject and that what he is teaching them must be what is important to know. If one gets a good grade, one has therefore necessarily learned something worth knowing. Where students do not accept the rationale, and feel a conflict between grades and learning, we have counted the incident as evidence of the existence of the GPA perspective.

Here is an extended statement of the problem by a successful student leader who himself had very high grades:

> There's an awful lot of work being done up here for the wrong reason. I don't exactly know how to put it, but people are going through here and not learning anything at all. Of course, there are a lot of your classes where you can't really learn anything at all. . . . There's a terrific pressure on everybody here to get good grades. It's very important. They tell you that when you come in, we tell our own pledges that. We have to, because it's true. And yet there are a lot of courses where you can learn what's necessary to get the grade and when you come out of the class you don't know anything at all. You haven't learned a damn thing, really.
>
> In fact, if you try to really learn something, it would handicap you as far as getting a grade goes. And grades are important. . . .
>
> And, you see, it says in the catalog, if you read it, that C is a satisfactory grade. Well, do they mean that or don't they? Actually it's the minimum

grade here. But it's supposed to be a satisfactory grade. OK. Supposing you wanted to work on something in your own way and didn't mind if you got a C. Well, if C was really a satisfactory grade it wouldn't hurt you any. But that's not the truth. C is just barely passing. The most satisfactory thing is an A, and next is a B.

The grading systems are so cockeyed around here you can't tell what's going on. One guy does it this way and another guy does it that way and, as I say, in a lot of these courses the only thing you can do is get in there and memorize a lot of facts. I've done that myself. I've gone into classes where that's all you could do is memorize . . . memorize and memorize. And then you go in to take the final and you put it all down on the paper, everything you've memorized, and then you forget it. You walk out of the class and your mind is purged. Perfectly clean. There's nothing in it. Someone asks you the next week what you learned in the class and you couldn't tell them anything because you didn't learn anything.

There are a lot of guys around here who are very expert at doing that. They can take any course and learn what has to be learned and get through the course with an A. And yet, I don't think those guys are really that smart, not to me anyway. In my opinion there are plenty of people around here who have much greater potential and they just haven't found the classes where you can use it . . . We've got these kids coming in and I don't know what it is, they're not interested themselves in accumulating knowledge for its own sake or because it will be of any use to them. All they want to do is get a grade. Now, of course, grades are important. We tell them [pledges] to go out and get that grade. What else can you tell them? It's very important for the house and it's important for them to get the grade. They want to be offered those good jobs when they graduate. I don't blame them. I would myself. I've always tried to get high grades and I've done pretty well.

February, 1961, fraternity senior

This articulate student has presented most of the major themes of this aspect of the perspective, themes that recur more briefly in statements by others: Grades are important, for many reasons; one can get good grades without learning; indeed, trying to learn may interfere with grade-getting; the point of view is passed on in his fraternity. He denies other aspects of the GPA perspective that we consider later; for instance, he does not believe that grades really measure a person's worth. And yet he accepts the main outlines of the perspective, recognizing that grades are important and orienting his own activity and that of his house toward them.

Let us consider some more specific instances of the conflict. A student planning graduate work in one of the social sciences had read, before arriving at KU, many standard works in the field. He acquired a number of current volumes that he intended to read during his freshman year, but found that his course in introductory anthropology interfered with his plans:

> I got a B in the anthropology exam. I can't really afford to get that and besides it kind of hurts my pride. . . . We've got this Ashley Montague book. It's a lousy book. I don't even know why they assign it. And there's a lot of stuff in it that is just wrong. In fact, the instructor said so himself in class. He'll mention something it says in the book and then say that Ashley Montague is wrong about that. Well, naturally I didn't pay much attention to that and didn't read it carefully. I had read it quite a while ago. And then the test comes, and what do you think? Practically every question on it is straight out of Ashley Montague.
>
> A couple of them said, "Contrary to what was said in the lecture, Ashley Montague holds that . . .", for instance, that New World monkeys are descended from Old World monkeys. Well, then you were supposed to say whether that was true or false. Well, I didn't know whether Ashley Montague said that or not. I hadn't read the book in a long time. How could I remember anything like that? And I hadn't bothered to read it for the exam. In fact, I read a couple of chapters in *Anthropology Today* instead. But I can see I'm going to have to concentrate on reading all the assignments because that's what they give tests on. I don't think I'm ever going to get through *Anthropology Today* at this rate.
>
> *October, 1959, independent freshman man*

(The instructor cannot win. If he had satisfied this student by asking no questions on the assigned reading, others would have complained bitterly that he was "unfair.")

A student can choose learning over grades, but only if he is willing to suffer the consequences. One student, who planned a career in a field where successful performance in college was not a prerequisite, was willing to take the chance:

> When I was in high school, I think I was a senior or a junior, I can't remember, I ran across this word "existentialism." Well, I wondered what it meant, so I looked it up in the dictionary and that didn't do me much good. So I went out and bought a book and that led me to another book and I read through all of that stuff. And now I've got a whole shelf full of books there, Kierkegaard and all those people. I don't have to tell you their names and, well, here's the kind of thing I would do. I would sit in my biology class in high school and read Nietzsche. I got that book and I carried it to biology with me and every day I'd hide it in my notebook and read that all through biology class. Well, I didn't learn any biology, but I learned a lot of philosophy. That's the way I am, I can't seem to get my mind organized to fit into these patterns they have here. Now most people do it because they want to get a good grade in the course, but that doesn't mean anything to me.
>
> *May, 1961, independent sophomore man*

Something of the process by which students come to feel that they will have to concentrate on getting grades instead of the substance of a course is revealed in the following incident, in which a student decides that he will have to substitute rote learning for real comprehension of the material:

> While I was interviewing in a fraternity house, a freshman said to the older student I was talking to that he was having a lot of trouble with his trigonometry course. He said that he could get it by memorizing it but he didn't want to do that, he didn't think it was right. He wanted to understand it but he just couldn't for the life of him understand why certain things were the way they were. Why, for example, was a sine defined as the ratio between this angle and that angle? He couldn't understand that at all. The older student tried to explain to him that it was a matter of definition, but he couldn't understand that point even though the older fellow tried to explain it several times. Finally he said with evident disgust that he just might have to give up trying to understand it and memorize it, just in order to get a decent grade, because this way he was having a lot of trouble and not doing well on the examinations.
>
> *October, 1959, fraternity freshman and sophomore*

In another version of this aspect of the perspective, some students come to feel that many of their extra-academic activities are actually more educational than the activities designed to educate them. For instance, an occasional student, after listening to or participating in a bull session, made a remark like the one made by a fraternity pledge after an evening listening to some of the older members talking about intellectual topics with the observer. When the observer apologized for taking up his time and disrupting his studying, he answered, "Heck, no. I learned more this evening just listening to you guys talk about art than I've learned thus far in any of my courses."

Finally, we note that some students take a very moral stand in separating those activities that are appropriate when one is pursuing grades from those appropriate when one is interested in learning for its own sake. A student in danger of failing made the point:

> Fulton was reading *Crime and Punishment*. He was about thirty pages into it and said, "Jesus Christ, this is a morbid book." I said, "Yeah, a lot of people think that." He said, "It's a long son-of-a-bitch, too." I said, "It certainly is." Fulton said, "Well, I sure hope I get it finished." I said, "Why don't you get one of those digests of famous novels and read that instead?" Fulton looked absolutely shocked and said, "Oh, no, I read for enjoyment. I read because I like to read these books. The only time I use one of those digests is when I have to write a book report. That's different."
>
> *May, 1960, independent sophomore man*

CHAPTER **5**

DEFINITION OF THE SITUATION:
FACULTY-STUDENT INTERACTION

The student, pursuing his academic goals in the larger community of the university, defines his situation as one in which he must do well by getting grades sufficiently high for his own purposes, however he has come to define these. He approaches his experience in each classroom with this definition in mind and searches for cues that tell him what kind of place the class is in which to pursue that objective. The realities of the situation lead him to define his classes as places in which he can get the grades he wants by performing as the teacher wants him to. The student gets his grades from the instructors for whose courses he has registered, and he earns them by working for them, by fulfilling in one way or another and at one or another level of proficiency the reqiurements the instructor sets for the course. In doing so, he "earns his living" as a member of the campus community. The more proficient his performance, the higher the resulting grades.

This view of classroom interaction defines the teaching situation as an exchange of rewards for performance, rather than as some kind of "educational process." Because it is so much at odds with more conventional academic conceptions of classroom interaction, we discuss, in a later section of the chapter, our reasons for not accepting those views.

THE CLASSROOM CONTRACT

If the classroom is the workplace in which grades, the money of the college community, are exchanged for academic performance, it may be useful to extend our economic metaphor a step further and suggest that there is an agreement between teachers and students, analogous to the labor contract in the workplace, on the terms of the exchange. And there is such a contract—announced, perhaps bargained over, and fulfilled in the course of the semester as teachers and students interact in and out of the classroom. Teachers may be unaware of the terms of the contract, may not realize that their statements about how grades will be assigned are regarded by students as binding commitments. But students define their relationship with professors as one in which professors contract to reward performance in predictable ways. They devote much effort to discovering the terms of the contract and to trying to hold up their end of it, as they understand it, by appropriate academic performance.

Students decide what the terms of the contract are by observing and interpreting the words and actions of the teacher as the semester goes on. A class, for them, is not a series of isolated encounters, but rather a connected sequence of events extending over four and a half months. During that period, they engage in two simultaneous enterprises. They search for cues that, properly interpreted, will yield an understanding of what the teacher will demand in return for a given grade. At the same time, they attempt to do the things they have decided are important to get the grade they want.

Students infer the terms of the contract, in part, from the professor's general statement of what is required. He (or his assistants) may, at the beginning of the course, explain the number and kind of examinations and outside assignments required, the kind of response required in the classroom, and the contribution of each to the final grade. Some professors give little information, perhaps from laziness or forgetfulness or because they find the whole matter distasteful.

As the semester goes on, the professor's actions furnish further cues. He may praise some kinds of classroom activity and punish (if only with ridicule) others. Some students get better grades on an assignment or test than others, and students compare high-scoring papers with their own to see what kind of answers the professor prefers. When he "goes over" the test or paper in class, he may reveal further what he regards as an acceptable or superior performance. He may, for instance, explain why he will accept one answer to a question as correct but not another, and thus give the students information from which to deduce what he will accept on future examinations. All these actions give specificity to the general statements he has already made and thus define the terms of the contract more precisely.

If neither the words nor the actions of the professor or his assistants give sufficient information, students may find out the terms of the contract by interrogating other students about how the professor has acted in the past or how professors like him (others of the same rank, perhaps, or members of the same department) typically act. As we shall see later, searching for this kind of information is a common expression of the GPA perspective.

The power to define the terms of the contract lies largely in the instructor's hands. Students may argue over them or, in extreme cases, complain to a department head or dean. But they understand that, although they may make the instructor uncomfortable, they have no formal means of influencing the standards he sets for their performance. It is in such ways that the abstract idea of subjection occurs as a concrete reality in the student's daily life.

Students also believe (and their experience justifies the belief) that instructors vary greatly in the number and kind of demands they make for academic performance. Students therefore never assume that they know with certainty what an instructor wants of them; they suspect instead that every class will be different and that they can only be certain of what is expected after they have amassed a great deal of evidence, if at all.

However the terms of the contract are arrived at and communicated, the important point is that students define it as an agreement that is binding (insofar as its terms are clearly known) on the professor as well as on them: they expect him to recognize its binding character. Should he, in their view, fail to live up to his end of the bargain by ignoring or changing any provisions of the agreement, they will be angry and upset. Since they often "construct" the terms of the agreement out of an analysis of what may be offhand remarks by the instructor, he may be quite unaware that such a binding commitment has been attributed to him and may well violate it unintentionally. Indeed, he would probably refuse to agree to its terms in the first place if the bargaining were more explicit.[1]

Faculty typically have a quite different view of their bargain with students, though it too is implicit, seldom communicated directly to students. In their view, students either do or do not have the ability to learn what is being taught (however that ability is conceived or measured). Those who do not have the ability must be written off as hopeless, but (because of entrance requirements) they are presumably a small number. Among the able students, however, some do not do as well as their ability would permit because they are insufficiently "interested" or "motivated." Here is the faculty's version of the classroom bargain: every stu-

---

[1] Similar student conceptions are described in Carl Werthman, "Delinquents in Schools: A Test for the Legitimacy of Authority," *Berkeley Journal of Sociology*, 8 (1963), pp. 39–60; and Howard S. Becker, Blanche Geer, Everett C. Hughes, and Anselm L. Strauss, *Boys in White: Student Culture in Medical School* (Chicago: University of Chicago Press, 1961), pp. 158–187.

dent who can do the work should be interested enough to do so and to want to do so.

In taking this view, faculty fail to give sufficient weight to the pull of other interests. They do not see, for instance, that the student may not be able to afford any more interest in their course because he needs to devote time and effort to another course that is giving him more trouble. They see even less that the student feels he may not be able to afford any further interest because he thinks that other rewards available in organizational activity and personal relationships are equally important and that academic rewards must be balanced against that competition. They do not understand, in short, that from the student's point of view true maturity consists in striking that balance in a reasonable way.

It is probably incorrect to say, as we just have, that faculty do not know these things. We could put it more precisely by saying that what they do not see is the legitimacy students accord to this competition to the interest their course should generate, the legitimacy that arises from its grounding in the students' view of maturity. In this sense, they do not understand that able students do not feel free to strike the kind of bargain faculty members propose, for to do so would be immature and unbalanced. It is likely that students willing to make such a bargain are, from the student point of view, unbalanced, for they would be students who had no other interests, who were insensitive to the attraction of other worthwhile activities possible on campus.

Even though we are primarily concerned with students' definitions of the classroom situation, we rely, in the analysis that follows, largely on our own observations of classroom interaction, just as we relied in the preceding chapter on official documents to get at student definitions of the larger academic situation. We rely on our own observations rather than students' reports to us, which clearly would give their own definitions more adequately, for the same reason as before: students do not typically describe the situation but rather talk about their difficulties with it. Thus students do not often express the notion that the classroom is a place where grades are exchanged for academic performance. But they do talk about the difficulties involved in holding up their end of the exchange, in a way that implies that definition of the situation.

Though we rely mainly on our own descriptions of classroom situations, they are descriptions made from the student point of view. We describe those aspects of classroom interaction of which students took account in organizing their activities. We thus concentrate on those characteristics of the classroom that help or hinder the student in the pursuit of goals specified in the GPA perspective, the characteristics that affect his knowledge of the classroom contract and his ability to uphold his end of it.

Our descriptions of the classroom will thus be incomplete, even one-sided, reflecting what is of interest to students and leaving out many matters professors consider important. But they contain the important features of the student's effective environment, those that impinge on him directly and that he consciously defines as constraints, necessities, and situational imperatives.

We learned what students took cognizance of, first of all, by direct observation of their response to classroom events. We went to class with students whose acquaintance we had already made in some other way, asking them to suggest classes for us to visit that were particularly good or bad (on whatever basis they made the judgment) or asking if we could accompany them through a typical day of classes. Students ordinarily introduced us to the instructor before the class began and we then sat with the student, so that he could give us explanations of what was going on or make evaluative comments as the class proceeded.

We visited twenty-five classrooms, usually for an hour period (although some laboratory classes lasted two or three hours). Ten classes were introductory courses, mainly large freshman courses in popular subjects; the other fifteen were scattered through the remaining years. Ten of the courses were in social science (including education and business administration), eleven in the humanities, and four in natural science. It is a haphazard sample of all classes given, but we are largely interested in getting at the range of variation among classes rather than in establishing the relative frequency of classes of different kinds, so the defect is not serious. In any event, the sampling represents the idiosyncrasies of the students we visited classes with, rather than any systematic bias of our own.

In addition to direct observation of classroom interaction, we gathered data on student definitions of the classroom by recording what they said to one another in everyday conversation and what they said to us during interviews in the field. Discussion of classroom events is a commonplace of student conversations; indeed, the perspectives eventually put into practice in the classroom are developed and transmitted during such conversations. Combined with observation and interviewing in the classroom situation itself, this material allows us to get at student definitions of the situation.

Professors make explicit comments on what they expect of students only on rare occasions, such as at the beginning of the term or when an examination is handed back and discussed. Since we attended each class only once, it was a matter of luck if we happened to be present when such comments were made. Much of our analysis is based on more normal situations, in which teachers suggest what they want indirectly: by ignoring what some students say and responding interestedly to what others say, for example. We have quoted such fragments, as well as the more extensive examples we have, to indicate the nature of the material on which our analysis is based.

CLASSROOM AND COURSE REQUIREMENTS

Once the student sees the class as the place in which he gets, in exchange for his academic performance, the grades he has earlier defined as the major rewards for academic work, he can define particular aspects of the classroom situation as capable of creating problems, of making it easy or difficult for him to achieve what he wants. Students often define the following as problematic: the formal structure of student-teacher interaction, which affects the student's ability to get adequate information about the terms on which grades will be awarded; the character of the formal requirements and the clarity with which they are communicated in class, which have the same effect; the nature of the behavior required in class; and the ease with which required knowledge of the subject can be acquired in class.

Class Organization. Classes vary in size from lectures attended by several hundred students to seminarlike discussion groups of eight or ten. They also vary, concomitantly, in the kind of formal relation that exists between teacher and pupil. In the largest classes, the relation is quite formal, mediated by a staff of teaching assistants. The professor lectures to the assembled group of several hundred, and discussions of the lectures and assigned readings take place in smaller groups led by graduate teaching assistants responsible to the professor. The teaching assistants usually grade examinations and term papers as well and confer with students who need help or advice. Many of the most popular introductory courses are organized this way.

At the other extreme, specialized courses in advanced areas of a subject, ordinarily taken by junior and senior departmental majors, are much smaller. The instructor may lecture, but discussion and interchange between him and his students are more likely. There are no teaching assistants, and students deal directly with the professor when they have problems with the material or wish to discuss examinations and papers (which he probably grades himself).

Variation in size and formality affects the student's access to the professor, which in turn affects his ability to get the information he may need on what is required and to get such further information as he requires on the substantive material covered in the course. In the large lecture course, communication is one-way, with little opportunity for the student to question the professor or to observe his response to statements and thus infer how he will respond to particular answers on an examination or to some specific point of view in a paper. He must be content with secondhand information gleaned from graduate assistants. (Graduate student information is secondhand in the sense that, though the assistants may indeed participate in grading the exam, it is likely to have been prepared by the instructor; furthermore, final decisions as to the "correct" answers will also be made by the instructor. The assistant, particularly as the student sees it, cannot be the ultimate source of information on these points.) The student in the small class, on the other hand, has the advantage of face-to-face contact with the professor, can ask direct questions, and can make continuous observations of his classroom responses to what students say and do.

Variation in size and formality are typically, though not necessarily, related to variations in the other dimensions of classroom interaction. Thus large classes often have more clearly stated formal requirements, require very little of the student in the classroom, and make it hard for him to get the information he needs for a passing grade. But these are only empirical regularities, not necessary connections.

Formal Requirements. The formal requirements of a course specify the minimal actions a student must take to earn a passing grade: the examinations, assignments, and participation in classroom activities. In some classes a great many small assignments are given; in others, the instructor requires only a few large pieces of work. The scheduling of due dates for assignments and tests varies greatly, too, though it is likely to be tied to the rhythm of midsemester and semester end. The requirements of the course also include the criteria by which performance will be judged, the standards according to which each performance will be assigned a grade.

Instructors vary in the number of components they use in calculating the student's grade, in the weight they give each, and in the clarity with which standards of performance are defined. Some classes have a fixed schedule of payments for different kinds of work. This reaches its extreme, perhaps, in one of the large freshman-sophomore courses, in which the student earns an A by accumulating, let us say, 500 points during the semester. A schedule lists a large number of assignments and examinations for the semester and tells how many points will be given for each one. If he accumulates the 500 points in any combination of assignments, he gets an A. Similar minima are set for each of the other grades.

Other instructors do not carry things so far. They may specify that a third of the grade will depend on the paper and the other two thirds on examinations, or some such similar division. They often, however, leave unanswered what may appear to be minor technical questions about how grades are calculated. For instance, will grades from several examinations given during the semester be averaged or will the final examination be given more weight than midterms and quizzes? Must the student achieve a certain minimum on both the test and paper or can he redeem a failing paper with an above-average examination score? In grading a paper, how much weight will the instructor give to content and how much to such formal details of presentation as spelling, punctuation, and neatness?

Even more important, from the student's point of view, instructors leave similar ambiguities in their statement of what will constitute acceptable performance. In some subjects, as they are conventionally taught, assignments require the student to discover the one right answer to a problem. Mathematics and analytic chemistry probably approach this extreme. In other subjects, such as the humanities and social sciences, there are a variety of ways of performing acceptably, of convincing the professor that you know what you are supposed to know. An English theme done in any of a number of ways can still earn an A (though not if it contains spelling and punctuation errors). In fields that contain competing but equally defensible points of view, some instructors may demand that students accept their interpretation of controversial issues; others encourage (and reward with high grades) the expression of differing points of view.

In short, when a student first enters a class he does not know what will be required of him and on what basis his performance will be judged, even though the instructor may have attempted to give an explicit account of these matters. The ambiguity, however, decreases as the course continues. As the instructor grades early assignments and tests, he communicates more precisely the criteria he is using, either explicitly or by the reasoning he uses to justify his decisions. Here are two examples of professors explaining what they want, taken from classes in which we happened to be present on the day an assignment or test was returned:

Now the test itself is supposed to serve a pedagogical purpose. In fact, no test is any good if it doesn't serve that kind of purpose. Your first test, if you remember, was meant to say to you, "You'd better read Jones [the course text]." And this test says, "Yes, read Jones, but read Smith [a book of supplementary readings] too." In other words, between these two tests you should have learned that I want you to read your text and I want you to go through these readings pretty carefully because most of the questions were based on the readings rather than on Jones.

Now here are some hints. For instance, when you read these readings, what do you do? I think what you ought to be doing is to read through it and understand not just the conclusions the man arrives at but how he got there. What is his logic? What kind of argument does he make for his position? *Classroom observation, introductory course for juniors and seniors, March, 1961*

I looked at those examination papers. I didn't get them all graded, but some of you in here didn't do so well. . . . The highest score on the test was sixty and that's not good enough. I am very disappointed in those formulae you were supposed to know. When I give your papers back I want you to take them home and use your books or anything else you have and get them right. [He began putting the problems on the board and working through them. There were ten, and each counted ten points. In discussing one question, he wrote a formula on the board.] That's what I wanted. However, nobody put that down, but you'll find it in your notes. You remember, I showed you how to do this. . . . I emphasized over and over again that this definition is the most important thing in the course. I should have counted fifty points on this question, but I didn't. But it will probably be on every test you get so you'd better learn it.

Classroom observation, introductory course, October, 1959

Some classes, however, give few clues as to what is expected. Thus an art instructor may require that a certain number of projects be finished, but not specify on what dates they are due. Furthermore, the student may complete the required number of projects and still get a low grade, although it is not clear what kind of performance would earn a higher grade. The instructor may not be exactly sure what kind of art object he wants the student to produce. Perhaps, at best, he would like the student to surprise him with something no one has ever thought of before. An art instructor explained his approach to an observer:

We are trying to loosen them up here; we're trying to be creative. The first project was to explore the possibilities there are in paper and to teach them something about design and also about construction, because if they are not well constructed they don't hold together. . . . The last thing we do in this class is to make a kite. Here construction is very important and we spend two days outside trying to fly them. Of course, they don't all fly but they make them in very unusual designs. The idea is not to stick to anything conservative or conventional.

Teacher of introductory art course, March, 1961

This means, in practice, that the student has little to go on in deciding what he should do to meet the requirements of the course. He may know that if his sculpture collapses he will not get a good grade, but he does not know what kind of sculpture that stands up will do the trick.

(He gets some help when the instructor displays works he considers good, though it is left to him to decide what is good about the work chosen for display.)

We will see in the next chapter how students respond to the ambiguities of professorial demands.

Classroom Behavior. Many different kinds of classroom behavior may be required of the student as he goes from class to class during the week. We do not speak here of the kind of knowledge the student must acquire in class if he is to be able to perform adequately on some later test, but rather of what he must do on the spot to give an adequate classroom performance. That is, the interaction in the classroom may require certain kinds of behavior if the student is to learn what he must eventually know; he may, for example, need the ability to take accurate notes rapidly. But we are concerned here with how he must behave in the classroom to give the professor a good impression of him or, at least, avoid making a bad impression. The instructor, we can suppose, has some notion of what should happen in the course of a class period; those students who help him to achieve what he wants will make a better impression on him than those who do not. How must the student play his part to make the class proceed as the instructor wants it to?

In the typical introductory course in many fields, hundreds of students assemble several times a week to listen to a professor lecture. The student participates only by listening. He asks no questions and is asked none. He need only attend to do what is required of him in class (and then only if attendance is taken). In classes of this kind a student can perform well even though he sleeps through every class. He can perform well, that is, *in class;* he may, because of his sleeping, miss items of information he will need for a paper or examination and thereby suffer. He will not, however, upset the instructor's conception of how the class hour is to progress, unless he is caught asleep. (The only classes in which our presence as observers seemed to cause trouble were the big lecture classes. Instructors often take attendance by seeing which students are absent from their assigned seats. By inadvertently taking the seat of an absent student, we could introduce inaccuracies into the tally.)

If we think of the classroom as a sort of stage, on which an hour's performance is to be given, we see that the student's part in a lecture course requires him to be nothing more than a spectator. In other kinds of classes, he is expected to take a more active part in the performance. One of the rules that generally governs classroom interaction is that there be no long silences; as in radio broadcasting, there must be no "dead air." The instructor can take advantage of this implicit rule to coerce student participation by being silent himself. Varying teaching techniques constitute different ways of using this feature of classroom interaction to involve the student in what is going on.

When the instructor, with a smaller class, uses a combination of lecture, Socratic questioning, and discussion, the student must do a good deal more. Much depends on how the instructor allocates questions and what use he makes of them.[2] In some classes, the instructor asks questions to bring out information that can be used to complete the performance he is giving. He asks the questions and then lets anyone volunteer an answer, often listening to several guesses before finding the one that will be useful to him and proceeding with his lecture.

> Professor Brown said that he had been told he could sell his house for $15,000. He said, "Do you suppose my house would be listed on the tax rolls at $15,000?" A number of students grunted negatively. He said, "What would it be listed at?" Students made various guesses ranging from one-seventh to one-half. He said, "Well, you're all right," and explained how the tax rate varied from one locality to another.
>
> *Classroom observation, senior class, February, 1961*

An instructor who uses this method is probably less interested in finding out what students know, for purposes of assessing their progress, than he is in eliciting statements that will contribute to his own performance and, consequently, does not call on students in a systematic way. The unprepared student does not suffer.

Some instructors use the combination of lecture and questioning more formally, calling on students in turn to supply answers from the knowledge they are supposed to be acquiring in the course, and keeping a record of who performs adequately and who does not. Their questions are designed to be used as an aid in grading, whatever other pedagogical purpose they may have.

The kind of material the student must produce to keep the class flowing varies greatly. In some classes, the instructor wants students to give answers they have learned in their reading or previous class discussions.

> The teacher said, "All right, today we're going to look at a few geometric problems." He then wrote out, first in words and then in numbers, some simple statements, such as: the sum of the angles of a triangle is 180 degrees, the perimeter of a rectangle is . . . , etc. Finally he drew a square and asked what the formula for its perimeter would be. A few boys murmured "Four S." The teacher ignored them and asked a student by name, who said, "S squared." The teacher shook his head and called on another student by name, who answered, "Four S," which he said was correct.
>
> *Classroom observation, remedial mathematics course, November, 1959*

[2] See John Holt's analysis of similar problems in elementary schools in *How Children Fail* (Boston: Pitman Publishing Co., 1964).

In others, he wants students to help him go through the steps of a formal argument, supplying items in a proof as he calls for them.

> The teacher began the class by saying, "At our last meeting we made an attempt to get at the theoretical scaffolding of how the data we had could be structured. Where shall we begin today?" A student said, "I don't see why the data on page two doesn't fit the theory on page one." The teacher said, "Five times out of a hundred this will happen by chance. But since it's an enduring social structure the norms will tend to come through." After further consideration of the data, he asked, "Does this set of facts bother you at all? High production and low internal rewards?" A student said he thought this might result "if the guys don't work with each other." The teacher asked, "Why?" Student: "Does this imply that management would rather have people on the line?" Teacher: "What do you think?"
>
> *Classroom observation, upper-level course, May, 1961*

In still other classes, the instructor encourages students to supply answers out of their general knowledge or to furnish examples, from their own experience, of the point under discussion, perhaps so that he can relate his remarks to something in their own lives.

> The professor lectured on role conflict, first making some general statements, then giving examples. One was that a boy in the Army might be served liquor when he had his uniform on although he was under age. The boys in the class began giving examples, not always to the point, about their experiences in the service in this regard. For instance, they talked about the fact that officers could always bring sufficient liquor on the base. A girl referred to the recent apprehension of an admiral for bringing in trunks of liquor from the Pacific. She said this man had been courtmartialed. One of the boys who had been talking about his experiences in the Navy, said, "Oh no he wasn't. He wasn't courtmartialed. They didn't do anything to him, I know. . . ." Eventually the professor began to lecture again.
>
> *Classroom observation, upper-level course, December, 1960*

Types of material acceptable or required in one class may be quite out of place in another. Thus a teacher who is interested in building an argument that leads to a particular conclusion will not welcome irrelevant points or examples, however interesting they may be in their own right. Conversely, a teacher who wants to stimulate discussion that will give students a new perspective on their own experience will be annoyed by what he might regard as premature attempts to synthesize some general point out of the discussion, no matter how brilliant the synthesis may be.

The form in which the student must produce the necessary answers also varies. At an extreme, we observed a class in which the instructor required students to give answers in complete, grammatically correct sentences. In most classes, colloquialisms and incomplete sentences are acceptable. In some, it almost appeared that the teacher preferred slang and informal expression, perhaps feeling that he was thus more likely to reach the level of the student's own experience.

One way to summarize our discussion is to say that every class has a culture of its own. To be sure, it is not the traditional wisdom of a primitive group; nor is it the way of life of such a transitory but relatively all-embracing group as the student body of a college or professional school. But it is a set of shared, gradually developed understandings about appropriate kinds of behavior in the classroom; it is, in the classic phrase, a design for living that small segment of one's life as a student. The culture of any classroom indicates to students who should talk, how much they should talk, what kinds of things they should say, how they should say them, and what the consequences are of behaving appropriately or otherwise. It is built up in the interaction between students and instructor, and between students themselves, but is ordinarily most strongly influenced by the instructor's demands, because it is the instructor who can reward or punish through grades.

Acquiring Knowledge. The formal requirements of the course and the customary form of classroom behavior combine to create a final set of professorial demands. The student must, under the conditions that characterize the classroom hour, acquire the knowledge he needs to satisfy the formal requirements, to pass the tests and adequately complete the other assignments. The demands for knowledge vary, as do the other demands, from class to class.

Different kinds of assignments call for different kinds of knowledge, even when the subject matter is the same. If the examination is made up of objective multiple-choice questions, the student must learn the exact phrasing given in the textbook or the lecture. Otherwise, he may be taken in by the alternatives that are deliberately worded to be almost but not quite right and miss the "one best answer" he is supposed to check. If, on the other hand, the examination consists of essay questions, the student need not worry about details of phrasing, but must instead have a broad grasp of the topic, a knowledge of details, and the ability to relate the two in a way that makes sense to the instructor. He needs, in addition, skills in writing and organization that should already have been acquired elsewhere.

Finally, the student must acquire the knowledge he needs under the conditions created by classroom culture. If classroom interaction characteristically consists of a sharing of personal experiences, for example, the job of finding out what point the teacher wants students to remember for later use may be a difficult one. The job is much easier when the teacher makes the point clear and refuses to let class discussion stray far from it.

In a lecture course, the professor's style of lecturing is the chief variable that determines how difficult it is to acquire the necessary knowledge. Some lecturers ramble, digress, and in general "make it difficult to take notes." Others present a clearly outlined body of material, dictating important ideas slowly enough for students to take them down verbatim and sometimes actually presenting, on the board or otherwise, a topical outline that gives the main points of the lecture in the proper order and relationship. A lecturer can make the student's job of acquiring the necessary knowledge easier if he makes a practice, as did one lecturer we observed, of indicating clearly which material in his lecture is necessary and which extraneous: "This is just an illustration. I don't care if you know anything about this or not."

ALTERNATIVE VIEWS OF THE TEACHER–STUDENT RELATION

We recognize that to view classes and academic work as a matter of exchange and contract, as we have in this chapter, will be considered by most educators as crass and belittling. To think of course work and the intellectual interchange of the classroom simply as the environmental context of grade-getting seems to slight the true functions of a college. Though few will deny that interaction between students and faculty has something of the economic character we have ascribed to it, few will willingly accept this as the major aspect of classroom interaction and accordingly will find students unreasonable or immature if they give it their first attention. Let us consider briefly two alternative views of the student-faculty relation commonly held by teachers and indicate why we find them inadequate.[3]

One view sees the relation of the student to his courses as one in which information and skills are transmitted to the student. He comes to class and is presented with certain materials. Readings and exercises help him to acquire the appropriate information and skills; assignments and examinations test whether he has in fact acquired what he is supposed to have acquired. This view assumes that what the instructor would like the student to learn is what the course requires him to learn. If that is true, the course requires the student to acquire information in order to get a good grade.

But things do not quite work that way. Very frequently, the assignments and requirements attached to a given course do not require the student to learn the information and skills that the instructor wishes him to learn, but rather another set of skills more closely related to the examinations and assignments actually given. Faculty members often

---

[3] For a discussion of models of the student-teacher relationship, see Blanche Geer, "Teaching," *International Encyclopedia of Social Sciences*, Vol. 15, pp. 560–565.

complain that, even though their students get good enough grades on examinations, they have not really learned whatever it is the faculty member wants them to know. The difficulty is that of constructing examinations that will truly test what they are supposed to test. The English professor may want his students to acquire the ability to enjoy and analyze literature; but his examination requires them to learn names and dates. The mathematics professor may want his students to grasp and be able to use certain difficult mathematical concepts; but his examination requires them only to be able to solve certain kinds of problems, whether they understand the concepts or not. In short, even where instructors desire only to transmit information or skills to the student, the mission may not be accomplished because the instructor's actions (particularly his examinations), as the student interprets them, do not require the accumulation of the information he wants the student to have. Rather, the student may be forced by the situation, as he defines it, to learn something different in order to pass the examination and get a good grade.

Furthermore, as we have already noted, though faculty members think that all students able to do the work ought properly to be interested enough to do so, students feel that they must balance the demands of any one course against those of other courses and balance as well the demands of academic work against those emanating from other areas of college life. The student does not see his task simply as learning what he is supposed to learn, but as doing that in a context of competing demands he considers equally valid.

The second school of thought has a more ambitious view, seeing the true and important function of education as the transmission of values. In this view, information is not important; rather, the teacher wants to transform the student's way of looking at the world and judging it. In a slightly different form, the teacher asks that the student develop his personality while he is in college. The educational experience—both in the classroom and outside of it—provides an opportunity for the student to learn to know himself better and to deal with himself and the world more adequately. In this view, the student must experience an unfolding of his personality, a liberation from conventional forms of thought, if he is to have gained anything from his college experience.

Insofar as this point of view states an ideal, we have no quarrel with it here (although, it may be said, this is no simple question). However, if it supposes that students really do acquire new values or experience an unfolding of their personalities as a consequence of their academic work, it is probably incorrect and certainly ignores the effect of course work as a constraint that must be satisfactorily dealt with if one is to do well in college.

Evidence that classes are not primarily forums in which opinions are exchanged and values shaped can be found in the many studies of the effect of course work on student attitudes. Both the Jacob report [4] and the review of the relevant literature by McKeachie [5] show that classwork in college tends to have little if any effect on student attitudes and values. Furthermore, varying methods of teaching also have little effect. This makes the proposition that students are deeply influenced by their course work less credible than it might otherwise be.

The proposition suffers a more serious setback when we consider the conditions under which students take courses. The theory assumes that students wander through the university freely, taking those courses to which they are drawn by their own needs and state of maturation. The student searches out those things he is psychologically ready for and, having been exposed to them, has experiences that powerfully affect his view of himself and the world.

Such a picture of the student is grossly in error. Students do not wander around freely picking and choosing among courses. On the contrary, in most colleges their choice of courses is severely restricted by the distribution requirements for all undergraduates and by the particular requirements for various majors. To graduate from the College of Liberal Arts and Sciences of the University of Kansas, a student must accumulate 124 credit hours. Of these, it is likely that three quarters or more will be prescribed in such a fashion that they cannot be freely chosen by the student. Thus a student majoring in English will have thirty-three credit hours available for courses that can be chosen without restrictions of any kind. But this is a very generous department. In physics, there are twenty-six elective credits possible, but all of these are subject to various restrictions, since the department directs that they must be chosen from among certain courses, most of them in the natural sciences. Many other departments similarly restrict the way elective credits can be used by suggesting lists of courses from which a major in their department should choose.

Bright students may have even less freedom to choose because they can, if they wish, take double and even triple majors. This exposes them to the demands of more than one department, so that their freedom to choose courses purely on the basis of their interest in them is even smaller than that of the average student. (A few students can get permission to take unusual combinations of courses for a major essentially of their own creation. But this is uncommon.) A student who wished to go

[4] P. E. Jacob, *Changing Values in College* (New York: Harper Bros., 1957).
[5] W. J. McKeachie, "Procedures and Techniques of Teaching: A Survey of Experimental Studies," in Nevitt Sanford, ed., *The American College* (New York: John Wiley and Sons, 1962), pp. 312–364.

where his need for new experience led him would probably have to take many extra courses to satisfy the requirements of the college and the department in which he eventually graduated.

The view that interaction between teacher and student affects students' values and personalities fails, finally, to give sufficient weight to the organizational context within which that interaction takes place. As we have seen, the system of grades and credits provides an institutional framework that instructors can use to reward those who learn to meet academic requirements and punish those who do not. Because the GPA is a relatively objective means of distributing sanctions and because the effect of the sanctions extends into so many other arenas of campus life, students can easily define it as the chief mark of academic success and consider striving for grades by attempting to meet academic requirements as the most appropriate course of action to pursue in their dealings with instructors.

But proponents of the view we are criticizing do not believe that important changes in students can be brought about through the use of external rewards, for the rewards that lead to personality and value change are presumed to be private and personal, unconnected with any immediate social profit. If they use sanctions at all in their effort to promote personal growth in students, they are likely to make use of such devices as shaming students who do not express ideas or opinions they consider desirable. But such devices, and the ends they are designed to promote, are personal and idiosyncratic, not tied in to any campus-wide system of reward. Thus they cannot be expected to have the desired effect on students' perspectives. A student may dislike being shamed in class, but the discomfort exists only in that class and has no effect on any of his concerns or activities beyond it.

We do not argue that nothing goes on in college classes beyond the exchange of the proper performance for a grade. But we do emphasize that the exchange of performance for grades is, formally and institutionally, what the class is about. Changes in personality or values may indeed take place, but they are not directly affected by the institutionalized system of value and reward. This no doubt accounts for the hostility that partisans of personality change in college generally display toward grading systems.

CHAPTER **6**

INFORMATION AND
THE ORGANIZATION OF ACTIVITY

In an institutional setting, we require information about what we are dealing with before we can take steps to deal with it. We must first learn the nature of the environment and what it demands of us, by what rules the institutional game is played, how various occupants of important positions in the institution will apply them, and what, on the basis of our own experience and that of others, will be the likely outcome of different lines of activity we might pursue.[1]

We must also know our own position in the structure of the institution. What kind of person am I, in the terms provided by the institutional context? Am I living up to what is expected of me? Am I doing my job, or are there some respects in which I am falling down?

The two kinds of information make it possible to plan a course of activity. Once a person has acquired them, he knows what he must do if he is to act successfully. In this chapter, we observe students as they go about the task of finding out what the rules are and where they stand with respect to them. Our data show that the kinds of information about academic work students consider important are those related to the GPA perspective. They are concerned, on the one hand, with finding out what the professor expects them to do in return for a "good grade." On the other hand, they want an accurate current appraisal of where they stand as measured by their GPA. In both cases, their actions reflect what we have described as the grade point average perspective; we consider each such instance to be evidence for the perspective's existence.

[1] For a discussion of this problem in a variety of other educational settings, see Blanche Geer et al., "Learning the Ropes," in *Among the People: Studies of the Urban Poor,* Irwin Deutscher and Elizabeth Thompson, eds. (New York: Basic Books, 1968).

80

SEEKING INFORMATION

As we have just seen, professors differ a great deal in what they require of students and, furthermore, are often vague and ambiguous in the way they state what they require. No student can ever be fully assured, when he enters a class for the first time, that he knows with certainty what he will have to do to earn the grade he desires. Even though the professor has been at the university long enough to have developed a "reputation" that describes what he wants, even though older students assure one that the requirements for a given course are well known and have not changed in years, one can never be certain that this will not be the year the professor decides to change his ways. Even though he gives what he regards as a full explanation of the requirements, students believe that disparities between what professors say and do are frequent enough for them to continue their search for information even after the professor has given his account, as he usually does, of the "mechanics" of the course: the schedule of assignments and tests and the grading procedures.

Students expressed this aspect of the GPA perspective in a number of ways. They often stated the necessity of discovering both formal and informal requirements and complained because they were unable to do so, or they explained in more general fashion how they found out what was required. In addition to statements students made both to us and to each other, we also had as evidence our observations of students actively seeking information on requirements from instructors or fellow students.

Students inquire directly of instructors or other university officials, seeking to clarify ambiguities in formally stated requirements or to discover additional requirements or contingencies the professor has left unstated. A formal statement, thought by the professor to cover all the necessary points, often fails to reveal all that students need to know to act efficiently in getting grades. Many freshman courses, for example, are offered in several forms—an Honors course for the best students and one or more courses at lower levels of difficulty for less able students. Many students wonder how the chances of getting an A vary among the different courses. An entering freshman asked, in a group discussion during Orientation Week:

"Is it true that you can't get an A if you are in that Math 21 course?" (Math 21 is the lowest-level regular college math course; students who perform exceptionally well on a placement examination may begin in Math 31 or 41, which cover much of the same material but at a higher level.)

[The University official conducting the discussion] looked rather blankly at the speaker for a moment and then he said, "I'm not sure I understand just what you mean." The boy continued, "Well, I mean I've heard that unless you are in those other math courses, what did you say they were—31 and 41—unless you're in those courses you can't get an A." [The University official assured them that a student had the same chance of getting an A no matter which of the freshman math courses he was in.]

July, 1960, entering freshman

Students often inquire, in a way that most faculty members find annoying, about the exact nature of assignments and tests. Every teacher has been subjected to such questions: "Are we responsible for the material in your lecture or only what's in the book?" "How long does the paper have to be?" "How many questions will be on the exam?" While they have little to do with the subject matter of the course, the questions probe for what students believe to be necessary items of information, without which it will be difficult to plan and organize academic effort.

We do not have sufficient material to make a detailed analysis of the use to which such information is put, but our earlier study of medical students suggests the direction in which such an analysis might proceed.[2] Students organize their studying around the cues furnished by the information they uncover, using strategies designed to counter the testing strategy adopted by the instructor. If, using examinations as an example, the instructor announces that an examination will consist of two essay questions, students may reason that the questions will call for broad interpretive answers, rather than detailed factual knowledge. They will then try to analyze the subject matter into a few major points and not bother to memorize details. Conversely, if the instructor announces a multiple-choice examination of 150 questions, students may reason that such an examination must concentrate on detail and thus devote their time to memorization. A full-scale study of the relation between professorial and student strategies with respect to examinations and other assignments is needed; we can only show here that students seek the information necessary to construct such strategies (and, later, that they orient their actions to winning such a strategic battle), and cannot give the details of the strategies they use.

In addition to seeking information about formal requirements, students also try to discover whether the instructor has tastes they should cater to or prejudices they should avoid arousing in preparing assignments and taking examinations. Students often think that the way a professor assigns grades depends not only on how well the students learn

2 See Howard S. Becker, Blanche Geer, Everett C. Hughes, and Anselm L. Strauss, *Boys in White: Student Culture in Medical School* (Chicago: University of Chicago Press, 1961), pp. 121–122.

their lessons but also on whether their work is in agreement with him in matters of opinion as well as matters of fact. Some students thought, for instance, that their mark on an English theme might reflect the instructor's personal opinion on the subject discussed rather than accuracy in spelling, proper punctuation, good organization, and the other requisites of a well-written theme. Insofar as students believe this, they find it necessary to search out those professorial idiosyncrasies that may affect their grade.

I can't get on to that son-of-a-bitch [the English instructor]. The first theme was absolutely perfect in spelling and grammar, not a single mistake in it, and I got an F. He had just written all over it "ideas," meaning he didn't like my ideas. [Instructors may criticize a theme for ideas that are overly simple, trite or poorly developed, but not on the grounds that the ideas disagree with their own.] Well, OK, so I tried again on the next theme. There was one spelling error and one misplaced comma, and the same thing—he had written "ideas" all over it. He didn't like my ideas again so I got another F. I'm just going to have to go in and talk to him, that's all there is to it, because I can't figure out what kind of ideas he does like. But I'm going to have to figure it out or I'll be out of luck.

April, 1960, independent sophomore man

Students also get information from one another, either from advanced students familiar with the requirements of various courses and professors or from students currently taking the same course. The information may be passed on in an unofficial tutorial (of the kind fraternities often arrange), it may be taken from a living group's file of old exams and term papers, or it may be distilled out of the pooled bits of information gathered by a number of students in the same course.

Students may simply ask each other for the details of an assignment whose announcement they missed. How long, for example, should the English theme be? How will the final grade be calculated? How much will each item of work count? What is the exam going to cover? If the information is not available from the professor, they try to get it from one another. When the professor fails to give sufficient information on the details of how he will grade or what material he regards as important, students pool their information. In the following example, two students taking different sections of the same course compare notes, trying to discover how the instructor is going to make up their final grade. Some of their comments indicate how they use the information to calculate a profitable allocation of their time and effort.

Ken said, "I didn't do too good on the first test. I got an 88, which means I missed an A by about two points. But then I got 95 on the second test. You see, what I'm hoping for is that he'll follow the procedure he used in the past, which is if you've got an A going into the final you don't have to take the final. That'll give me a lot of extra time at the end of the semester."

Hank said, "Well, I think he totals the points up, over all the tests, so if you were just two points down on the first one you can easily make it up someplace else."

Ken said, "Well, I already have. But, you see, he didn't say for sure that he was going to do it that way. I know they have done it that way in the past but I don't know if he's going to do it that way this time."

Hank said, "Oh, yes. He said so definitely in our class."

Ken said, "Well, he kind of hinted at it in our class. Did he really say definitely in your class?" Hank said yes and Ken lifted his arms up in the air and shouted "Hallelujah!"

. . . Hank asked Ken what was likely to be on the final in Geology and on the next exam too. Ken said that he had heard that you were going to have to know all about faults. Hank said, "Is the next exam going to cover everything we have had so far or just the material from the last exam to this one?"

Ken said, "I think it's going to repeat a lot from the last exam. It'll be for the whole semester really."

Hank made a face and said, "Boy, that's terrible. What kind of questions do they ask?"

Ken said, "Well, what they'll do is present you with a diagram and then you have to figure out . . . you know, that it was sedimentary rock and then it was folded down deep and then it faulted and then it came to the surface and was eroded and then it was covered with something else. That kind of stuff."

January, 1961, two independent sophomore men

Students may also, like medical students,[3] try to decide by discussion among themselves which of the many possible interpretations of an assignment will be acceptable. The two freshmen girls in the following example do not decide what to do about a specific assignment so much as they decide on the criterion to use in making that judgment; the anxiety produced by a lack of information is evident:

Anne said, "And then the assignments they give can confuse me. I mean, I don't know what I have to learn here. They say 'Read Chapter 1.' All right, Chapter 1 is 20 pages long. How do I know what I'm supposed to remember with all that stuff. I don't know what kind of questions they're going to ask about it. I can't tell what to study."

Kathryn said, "I don't think that's so hard. I mean, it might be until the first quiz, but after that you can tell what kind of questions the professor is going to ask, and then you know what to study. You can usually tell pretty

3 Becker, Geer, Hughes and Strauss, *op. cit.*, pp. 135–157.

soon, I think. . . . Teachers ought to explain anything that isn't in the text-book that they want you to know, and that's all, then you know what it is you have to remember. You can usually begin to tell when you get the first quiz, though. That makes it a lot easier, I think."

Anne said, "Well, I can't tell yet, and it's got me worried, to tell you the truth."

September, 1959, two freshman girls

Relying on the first quiz for information is a common pattern, if only be-cause it gives relatively unequivocal information; by the questions he asks, the instructor reveals his intentions most clearly and resolves the ambiguities about what must be known that bother these freshmen.

Finally, in addition to getting information from instructors or one an-other, some students make use of deductive logic, constructing a "sys-tem." A "system" consists, in essence, of a hypothetical model of the in-structor's behavior that specifies how he makes up an examination, what he considers important, and what answers will please him. Students pre-dict, on the basis of their "system," the questions that will be asked on examinations and prepare themselves for those questions.

We did not investigate student "systems" in enough detail to know whether they are more reliable guides to action than are systems for playing the horses or roulette. It is not likely that they would be, because instructors may emphasize one thing in class and another on an examina-tion. Nevertheless, students make use of them. Some systems, such as that used by medical freshmen, are rationally constructed out of an anal-ysis of carefully checked information.[4] But systems, though deductive in form, are not necessarily rational strategies. They may be based on spec-ulation and intuition and may even be quite magical, as the following generalized discussion of how systems are constructed makes clear:

A student who had transferred as a junior from another university said, "It doesn't have anything to do with studying. It's just a matter of getting to know the system here and I'm not on to it yet, that's all there is to that. Hell, down where I was before all I had to do was get one quiz from an instructor and then I could tell you what was in every other exam he gave so I didn't study at all. Two days before the exam I'd hit the book and run through it and mark all the things I knew he was going to ask and read up on that and I'd be in. Never had any trouble at all. I'm just not on to this system here yet, but I'll get on to it, don't you worry. . . ."

The observer said, "You'll have to explain to me how you do that."

Jim said, "Well, I'm not so sure I can. It's more like intuition or something. I don't know if I could explain it, but I sure as hell could do it."

February, 1960, independent junior man

4 *Ibid.*, pp. 158–184.

Once a student has convinced himself that his system accurately predicts professorial behavior, he is apt to feel that the teacher *ought* to grade and examine as the system predicts and to be outraged when the professor, perhaps following a system of his own, does something unpredictable:

> You know something? The reason I really took this anthropology course was I heard they give multiple-choice examinations. I figure I can take any multiple-choice examination and get away with it. . . . But this guy that's teaching this course does it differently. He really screwed me up. . . . Here's what he does. There could be more than one right answer to a question. He'll give you five choices and they might all be right so you get five points for that question, one point for each one you mark correctly and one point for each one you leave blank correctly and you lose a point for every one that you leave blank and every one that you fill in wrong. I can usually do pretty good at figuring out which ones are the really wrong answers in a regular multiple-choice exam, but in this one you can't take it for granted that a certain number of them are wrong. You know what I mean. You can usually figure that two or three of them are completely wrong, so then you've narrowed the chance of making a mistake down. It doesn't do any good this way. He's a very bright guy to think that up but he's sure hanging me up.
>
> *March, 1960, freshman independent man*

(This aspect of the GPA perspective tends to penalize the conscientious teacher who attempts to improve his course or add more up-to-date materials to it. Every effort at innovation undoes those aspects of student systems that depend on professorial inertia for their predictive power.)

The information students acquire, wherever it comes from, may be inaccurate. Professors may give incomplete or ambiguous answers to questions; students may assess professorial prejudices and idiosyncrasies incorrectly. Information from other students has all these defects and the further one of being secondhand and likely to have been distorted in transmission. Systems are either speculative or based on information gathered in one of these possibly faulty ways.

We do not insist that the information students secure is accurate. We argue only that they seek information on what they must do to satisfy the teacher's demands and that their information-seeking is an expression of the GPA perspective, a kind of activity required of them because professors do not, left to themselves, give sufficient information on which to base one's allocation of academic effort.

The conventional academic system has a built-in irremediable conflict. Professors do not like students to seek information of the kind we have described; that seems to them a misdirection of effort and curiosity that might better be devoted to the content of the course. But students are constrained to engage in information-seeking activities by the importance of grades and the ambiguity of professorial statements about how they may be achieved. The conflict might be averted if professors gave more detailed and less ambiguous directions on these points. Some instructors attempt this. The staff of the freshman English course, for instance, issues a booklet that tries to be extremely explicit about what constitutes an acceptable performance, even giving samples of good, bad, and average themes. But students do not regard this information as sufficient and search for more. What the faculty would have to do to satisfy their desire for information would be to give information of such detail and precision that the function of examinations and assignments as measures of student ability would be destroyed, for they would measure only the ability to memorize the material the faculty had provided. To provide anything less precise preserves the present arrangement, although at a different level, and maintains the present conflict.

KNOWING ONE'S GPA

If grades and grade point averages are important for the student's present and future campus life, he must know what they are. He cannot plan his actions without knowing what options have been or will be opened to him or closed off by his grades. He must know where he stands already—how much he has in his bank account, so to speak—and where he will probably stand at the end of the current semester—what he can estimate his current income to be. His predictions of what is likely to happen provide the basis for allocation of future efforts, along lines suggested by the information he has acquired about requirements. A variety of student statements and actions expressed this aspect of the GPA perspective and furnished evidence for its existence.

Students exhibited to us, again and again, a great familiarity with their grade point averages, past and future, current and cumulative. Many students, for instance, can, even as seniors, say what their average has been every semester of their school career. As an example, a campus leader, in the course of an interview, told us he had had an average of 2.6 for his first semester, and went on:

> As a matter of fact, I improved on those every semester. I had a 2.8 the second semester, then I had a 3.0 all through my sophomore and junior years. Last semester I went down to a 2.8 again. I got a B in history. I don't know how I will make out this semester.
>
> *April, 1960, senior fraternity man*

Not all of our evidence, of course, consists of such impressive mnemonic displays. We were actually very impressed by how often students, in casual conversation, were able to state their GPA to two decimal places. We were also impressed when a common (though by no means the only) answer to our intentionally vague opening question "How are you doing?" or "How are things?" was for the student to give his grade point average for the last or the current semester. (They might, of course, have responded to such a vague inquiry in any of a variety of other ways, so that their choice of grades and grade point averages as an appropriate answer takes on some significance. They might have spoken of their health, of their love life, or of organizational matters of many kinds.)

To know one's past GPA, one only needs a good memory. But students also "know" their average for the semester not yet completed, sometimes even before midterm advisory grades are announced and certainly afterward. They do this by calculating, on the basis of the instructor's evaluation of the course work they have already done, what their final grade in each course will be if they continue working at the same level, and what kind of average the combined grades will yield.

Students usually have some idea of how they stand in each of their courses at any given moment during the semester: "Well, I should have an A in political science and an A in speech, but I don't know for sure what I'll get in philosophy, and in English I think I'll be lucky if I get a B" (*January, 1961, independent freshman man*).

As students continue in their college careers, the semester's average becomes important less for itself and more for its contribution to the cumulative average. Some of our best examples come from students whose academic difficulties may endanger their chances of graduating. In the following case, the student calculates his chances in his present classes and relates his projection to his long-term troubles:

I [the observer] said, "By the way, how did you do on the midterms?" Brackett shook his head and said, "Not so goddamned well. Not really too bad, I got a couple of B's and a C and I got a D in philosophy, and I got an F in English. . . . My marks really aren't too bad but they're not too good, you know what I mean? . . .

"I'm not too worried about that D anyway. . . . [It] was just on the midterm and the midterm only counts one-fifth of the final grade. There's a final exam that counts two-fifths and the term paper that counts two-fifths, so if I can bring those up a little bit I'll be in. . . .

"I've got to get a C average this time. In fact, I've really got to get a little better than a C average." I said, "How do you figure that?"

He said, "I don't want to be in school forever. You see, you have to have an over-all C average to graduate over all your four years and I'm not going to do it unless I pull up above a C on some of my grades, because my other grades are so lousy. . . . I figure if I can keep it up around 1.2 from now on, which would be mostly C's and a B, I'll be in. But, for instance, if I get a D or two D's this time, say in English and philosophy, then that means that the next several semesters I'm going to have to get 1.4 or something like that. And that's a little bit rougher, boy, believe me, it's a little bit rougher." [5]

April, 1960, independent sophomore man

The projection of the current semester's grades becomes the basis for decisions about how to allocate one's efforts. The student puts his effort where it will do the most good. He may decide to concentrate on raising a particularly low grade in one course by devoting himself exclusively to it. Or he may be concerned with balancing his efforts in all courses, so that his GPA will be sufficiently high, for his own purposes, given the goals he is striving for in such other areas as organizational activity and personal relationships. If, for example, he should become so interested in one course that he failed to keep up in the rest of his program his over-all GPA might be very low; it is more to his advantage, under the formula from which the GPA is calculated, to keep grades in all courses relatively high than to do very well in one and poorly in the others. A normal program contains five courses (though there is a good deal of variation), so that the student has a number of elements to consider: the amount of effort required to raise a grade in a given course, the number of hours of credit for which he is taking the course, and the relative contribution to his GPA of a given amount of effort applied there as compared with the contribution of the same effort applied to some other course. The number of alternatives is large, and a wise choice requires careful calculation, calculation that might appear excessive, particularly to a faculty member relatively unaware of the demands made on the student in his other courses. In the following incident, the observer discusses with a very bright scholarship student how he will work for the rest of the semester:

"I don't know how I'm going to keep up my 2.5 average this way."

I said, "Is that what you intend to keep up?" He said, "It's what I have to keep up if I want to keep my scholarship." He began to calculate what marks he would need to get a 2.5 average and came to the conclusion that he could not get a B in math and a B in German too and keep up that average. . . . "Let's see, if I got a B in math and an A in German, how would that work out?" He calculated again and still this only came to 2.3 or something like that. He said, "I have to get an A in both those courses. Gee whiz!"

[5] This student's statement may seem reminiscent of the classical "gentleman's C" approach, but it is not. It is not that he is content to make a small effort in return for a C average, but rather that even with a very substantial effort he will be lucky to raise his average enough to graduate.

I said, "You're assuming that you'll get an A in all the other courses, is that it?" He said, "Oh, yeah. I don't think there'll be any trouble about that. They're all pretty easy for me, like anthropology and philosophy. I'm pretty sure they'll be easy. I haven't had any exams in them yet but I don't anticipate any trouble. . . . Oh, I left my hours in anthropology out. Now, let's see, if I got those in. . . ." He did it all over again and it came out this time that he could manage a B in either math or German, which were each five hour courses and thus counted heavily in the average. Then he remembered that there was something tricky about the credits for his Western Civilization course. He looked that up and discovered that that could be made to count for six hours credit if you did it right. He said, "Well, now, that makes a lot of difference. I know I'm going to get an A in math. I really enjoy that course too. Let's see how that would work out."

He made several more rapid calculations and eventually decided that he could get a B in both math and German and just barely have a 2.5 average if he got A in everything else, including the six hours of A in Western Civilization. This relieved him somewhat. That is, he felt no possibility at all that he would get B in both math and German.

He said, "Sure, the other way I could have gotten B's in those other courses, but those are the courses I'm sure to get A's in. This makes it a little better, but I still think I should make an A in at least one of those courses. . . ."

October, 1959, independent freshman man

All these calculations about grades might not necessarily reflect an interest in grades for the sake of grades. One could argue instead that students interested in learning the material a course has to offer see a low grade as an indication that they have failed to acquire something worthwhile they might well have acquired by more intensive study. We have already seen, however, that many students feel a distinct difficulty in trying to meet the requirements of a course and at the same time learning what is worthwhile in the content of the course. This tends to be most true of the better students, for whom getting a good grade is not in itself difficult, but simply time-consuming; they complain that if they had more time, free of course requirements, they could in fact learn more. For students not doing so well, who do not find getting a good grade so easy, the incidents just cited and the statements just quoted show that they are not worried about absorbing material for their own benefit, but rather about meeting the requirements in order to stay in school.

SUMMARY

We have seen, in this chapter and the one preceding it, how the relationship of subjection between students and faculty shapes some parts of the students' academic perspective. Instructors reward performance with grades, according to the terms of a varyingly explicit contract which, however, is established unilaterally, rather than being the consequence of bargaining and negotiation. (In this it resembles the kind of implicit contract that characterized the relations between industrial workers and managers in the days before organized labor was strong enough to force management to take its views into account.)

The most immediate consequence of students' subordinate position is that students find it necessary to seek information about faculty intentions and faculty practice in order to organize their own behavior toward the end of meeting faculty requirements. Furthermore, they seek information about the standing the faculty has assigned them, is assigning them, and will in the future assign them, as a means of judging how they have done and how they can expect to do and, therefore, what changes they had better make in their current practice to achieve a more desirable result.

The import of this, from a conventional faculty point of view, is that, given the importance of grades and the total control by faculty over the terms of their distribution, students cannot act as autonomous intellectuals, cannot pursue learning for its own sake, but must seek information on faculty behavior, present and prospective, before they can plan what they will do. In this sense, the relationship of subjection works against the commonly stated faculty goal of training students to be intellectually free and self-directing, and does so as a matter of structural logic rather than as a matter of human frailty, or student or faculty incompetence. (With regard to their own concerns, which go beyond the area of academic performance, students do of course exercise autonomy by deciding for themselves, in view of their other goals, how much weight they will give to the purely academic. But this kind of autonomy is not what faculty members ordinarily have in mind when they raise the question.)

CHAPTER 7

THE PURSUIT OF GRADES

A perspective contains, in addition to the cognitive elements we have just discussed, a set of actions. The group's members consider the actions appropriate and expedient—appropriate in that they are thought likely to achieve the goal and expedient in being adapted to the situation in which the goal must be sought.

In considering the actions contained in a perspective, we see most clearly how the basic framework of institutional practice, as members of the group perceive it and incorporate it into their definition of the situation, influences the perspective's character. Every action attempts to solve some problem that the participants define as created for them by the institution. Actions persist as part of the perspective because participants persistently perceive the institution as posing the same problems for them. They are solutions that group members have hit upon as a workable way of dealing with the environment as they define it.

The actions contained in the perspective cannot, however, be chosen freely from all those that suggest themselves. Group members do not consider their problems in isolation from one another. Instead, they view any particular problem in relation to all their other problems and choose a solution that will not only deal with the immediate difficulty but will also take account of other necessities in their overall situation. Thus an action that demands an inordinate amount of time and energy—time and energy to be taken from other equally pressing problems—is not an acceptable or workable solution.

INDIVIDUAL AND GROUP PROBLEMS AND ACTIONS

Some problems students have in dealing with the grading system come to each student separately. Each student takes his own collection of courses; though many students may share a similar program, relatively

92

few have to deal with exactly the same teachers or course and classroom requirements. In addition to having different specific requirements to meet, students vary in their ability to meet them. Furthermore, students have differing obligations, commitments, and ambitions outside the academic area, which influence both their need for "good grades" and their resources for obtaining them. Thus although student problems often are alike in their general features—many students, for instance, have the problem of having fallen behind in their work—the specific character of the problem varies from student to student.

Beyond this, these problems are individual in that the rewards for meeting the requirements and punishments for failing to meet them are distributed to individual students, rather than to groups. (A student's grades can, of course, have an effect on some shared problems of the groups he belongs to, as we shall see in a moment.) They are in the position of industrial workers who are paid an individual piece rate rather than being awarded a bonus based on the group's collective production. Individual problems of meeting academic requirements must be solved by the individual. But the techniques one uses and the ideas on which they are based are not individually constructed. Rather, students draw on the ideas current among their fellows (most often fellow members of their living group) and on the actions of others (again, usually fellow members of their living group) as they observe them in the course of their daily lives or become aware of them through conversation and discussion. They find support for what they do among other students to the degree that their actions conform to shared student understandings and make sense within the frame of reference assumed by those understandings.

Students, acting to solve their own problems, thus depend on and are influenced by the solutions that other students have worked out to *their* problems. If the problems are similar (and they inevitably are, because of the basic framework of academic practices that govern all classrooms and all students), students can develop a generalized set of actions, part of their academic perspective, to which their own particular actions can be referred. It is this sort of individual action based on group perspectives that we discuss in the first section of this chapter.[1]

---

[1] It would be possible to study the kinds of actions students devise in response to particular problems of academic work, in the same way that one might, as we have already suggested, study the kinds of information-seeking students devise in response to particular faculty practices, using the model of a game of strategy. We have not undertaken such a detailed analysis and confine ourselves to the generalized set of actions, developed in response to the generalized problems the college creates for all students, of which the particular actions developed for particular circumstances are special cases.

Other problems have a collective character. They affect the interests of a group, thus affecting all members of the group equally. Confronted with shared group problems, student groups develop forms of collective activity designed to solve those problems. On the KU campus, the organized living group is the most common locus of collective problems with academic work. All living groups have in one form or another the problem of maintaining or enhancing group prestige, and, as we have seen, the academic performance of the group plays an important part in its solution.

The actions taken by organized campus groups draw on group custom and tradition, handed down from one group of students to their successors, as well as on shared understandings developed *de novo*. Living groups can depend on custom in arriving at the proper action with respect to academic problems, as the individual cannot, for the living group persists and has continuity over the years. Group actions are of course subject, just as individual actions are, to the necessity of taking account of the situation as defined in the perspective and of the other kinds of problems the group faces. In analyzing organizational action, we have concentrated on the actions characteristic of highly organized groups, but have indicated as well how less organized groups sometimes, as best they can, approximate these.

We have interpreted each incident in our field notes that has the characteristics of any of the kinds of action, individual or group, to be described as evidence of the existence of the GPA perspective.

INDIVIDUAL ACTIONS

Having sized up their situation by discovering what needs to be done in each of their classes and projecting their semester GPA, students take action based on their definition of the importance of grades. Specifically, they express the GPA perspective when they take actions that have as their object getting a "good" grade, a grade sufficient for them in the light of their other grades, the total GPA they desire, and their other responsibilities and desires; in short, when they set their level and direction of effort with an eye to its effect on their GPA.

Student actions designed to get desired grades can take two forms. First, students may attempt to meet the requirements presented to them: they study and try to master the materials and skills they are supposed to acquire. But they may fail in that attempt or decide that they will fail if

An interesting study of differential responses to academic problems is reported in Jerome E. Singer, "The Use of Manipulative Strategies: Machiavellianism and Attractiveness," *Sociometry*, 27 (June, 1964), pp. 128–150. Singer's evidence shows, for instance, that grades are related to Machiavellianism among men and physical attractiveness among women.

that is all they do. Then they undertake other actions which, rather than being designed to meet the requirements, try to achieve the reward of grades through other, less legitimate means such as arguing with the instructor, "getting next to" him, or cheating. If they can do the job, they do it, putting their major efforts into academic work; if they cannot, they try to influence their grade in some other way.

Under some circumstances, students making use of the GPA perspective will, instead of raising their effort to meet requirements or looking for alternative forms of action, actually lower their level of effort substantially, leading (as we shall see) to the paradoxical result that an emphasis on grades leads to decreased effort to achieve them.

Doing the Job. Students study; they are supposed to. But they study harder at some times than at others, and the variation in effort is not a function of anything in the material they study itself, but rather of whether or not a term paper is due or an examination looms ahead. They study harder, too, when their GPA is lower than they would like it to be.

This may seem overly obvious and not necessarily connected with the perspective we are describing. After all, what do students come to college for if not to study? Why do we think it necessary to explain that they do so? Even if we were to grant this (ignoring the possibility that students might come to college for other reasons and have no intention of studying at all), it is still not obvious why a student should study in any particular rhythm, with peaks of effort at one time and periods of relaxation at another.

Consider the following example. A student says that his work is "piling up" on him, that he is "getting behind." Does he say this because he has come to college to study and learn and feels that he is not learning fast enough? On the contrary, he feels his work is "piling up" because he has a given amount of work to do in a specified amount of time; if he does not keep to a daily schedule, getting so much done every day, he will fall behind and have more to do on the following days.[2] He did not choose those amounts of work and time; because of the relationship of subjection in the academic area, they are set for him by the faculty. He must meet faculty demands because his grades will be based on how well he does just that.

We frequently found students who were not doing well working extremely hard. The poorer student probably studies longest; he has so much difficulty that he must devote all his time to his work. Here is an

---

[2] Howard S. Becker, Blanche Geer, Everett C. Hughes, and Anselm L. Strauss, *Boys In White: Student Culture in Medical School* (Chicago: University of Chicago Press, 1961), pp. 92–106.

example, from a conversation with a freshman girl on the verge of flunking out:

> Well, I start studying after dinner and I study all night until midnight and sometimes until one o'clock. And sometimes I start at six o'clock and just keep going right through. And I've been getting awfully tired, I think that's why I got that cold. Last weekend I went home and I slept thirteen hours until three o'clock in the afternoon.

November, 1959, freshman girl

Most instances are less dramatic. The student indicates that he has a great deal of work to do because of previous low grades and that he is doing what he thinks will be needed to improve them:

> I said to Harry, "How are things going with you?" He immediately replied, "Oh, I got a down slip [a midterm notice that one is likely to fail a course] in one of my courses and that's what I'm studying for now. I have a test in it tomorrow. . . ." I said, "How are your other courses going?" Harry replied, "They're OK, C's and B's. I'm doing all right in those and I think if I can work a little harder on this I can get it up to at least a C by the final. . . . Of course, I have no social life this semester and about all I'm doing is studying."

March, 1961, freshman independent man

Students need not be failing to behave this way; they may simply find it necessary to devote all their time to finishing required work in time to meet a deadline. Thus a student who had previously been quite prepared to engage in long conversations with the observer said: "Gee, you've caught me at a kind of bad time. I'm just trying to finish up a paper for Soc." (*January, 1961, senior man, scholarship hall.*) (Most of the few occasions when students were unwilling to talk to us involved similar situations; the student had too much work to do to allow him to take the time off.)

When devoting more time and effort to study does not work, students who want higher grades seek help. They may, for instance, take advantage of services organized by the faculty, such as tutorial instruction, the Reading Clinic or the University Counseling Center.

More commonly, however, students get help from other students or from files, maintained by their living group, of old examinations, term papers, and the like. During dinner at a fraternity house, an observer overheard the following:

> You know how to study for Professor Jones, now, do you? Did you follow the file? Well, if you follow that file the way the course is outlined, then you can't go wrong, because he's been giving that course in the same way for the past ten years. Just be sure that you memorize all of those definitions, just

the way that they are set up in the files, and you can't go wrong, you'll be sure of an A if you do.

November, 1959, junior fraternity man

Files of old examinations and papers are a tradition on many campuses. But students rely on fellow members of their living group for more than access to already accumulated files. They also ask for help in completing current assignments:

> The observer was lounging around in a student's room in the dormitory. . . . Long said, "[Bracket is] really busy in there. He's got a theme to turn in tomorrow and I don't think he's done anything on it yet." A little later Bracket arrived saying, "Does anybody know anything about Karl Marx? I've just run out of ideas. That's all there is to it. Where is Tucker? . . . He promised to give me an old term paper of his on Karl Marx that I could use." I said, "Johnny Bracket! Don't tell me that you would turn in somebody else's term paper?" He looked around quite seriously and said, "Oh, no. I didn't mean that. I just wanted to get some ideas out of it for the last two pages of my paper. I need about two more pages." Albright said, "I see. You would just copy the last two pages, is that it?" Bracket said, "Well, I wouldn't exactly copy them."

April, 1960, sophomore independent man

The pressure of assignments and the need to get grades thus push students to do the academic work assigned them. But, if pressure supplies a motive for work, its absence makes work less necessary. If the material need not be mastered now, but can be put off until later, the student may decide to work only as much as is required and no more. If he were sincerely interested in learning for its own sake, he would presumably continue to work on a topic until he lost interest in it or felt that he had learned enough to suit his purpose. But many students do only what is required of them:

> A student described having led a very extensive social life during the last semester, I said, "Did you get pretty good grades with all that?" He said, "I can't complain, I did just about as well as I expected." I said, "What was your grade point average?" He said, "2.6" [B plus]. I said, "Wow, that's pretty good, isn't it?" He said, "Yes, it is pretty good, it really could have been higher if I had applied myself more in English, but I didn't. I think 2.6 is plenty high enough. There's no harm in that. But I didn't have to apply myself to get it. And I didn't have any intention of applying myself. . . .
>
> "I don't mean to say that it was all a breeze. I had to put myself out occasionally. I had to get all those English themes in and so on. But frankly, with the exception of English, I didn't do any work at all the whole last month of school. I was caught up on all my other courses. I had done all the work for

the rest of the semester. And the only reason that I hadn't done it in English is that you couldn't tell ahead of time what kind of themes he would assign. Otherwise I would have done all of that too. I really had all the whole last month perfectly free to do whatever I wanted."

I said, "You might have gone out and read some things that weren't assigned. Did you do that?" He smiled very broadly and said, "No, sir, you don't catch me doing that. I'll do just as much as I have to to get the grades and that's all."

October, 1959, sophomore fraternity man

Students who take this point of view make it their business to discover just what is required so that they can do the minimum necessary for the GPA they want. As soon as they discover that some action that seems necessary for a grade in fact is not, they dispense with it, even giving up going to class when that can be managed without running afoul of rules about "cuts":

I don't know about these classes. I've got one class where the fellow lectured about one set of things and then gave us an exam on a completely different set of things out of the book. I really don't think I'm going to go to that class any more. I mean, what's the sense of sitting there and taking notes if he's going to ask questions straight out of the book? I might as well just read the book and let it go at that.

November, 1959, independent man, year in school unknown

The emphasis on what is required is reflected even in the interior decoration of student rooms. We repeatedly noticed that many students' bookshelves contained nothing but textbooks. Many other students, of course, had sizable collections of books that were only distantly related, if at all, to their course work. But a substantial number of students apparently had no use for books that would not be helpful in attempting to meet requirements.[3]

Illegitimate Actions. Some of the actions that students take in pursuit of grades would be regarded as illegitimate by most faculty members. Faculty believe that students should work as well as they are able, and that they will do so if the faculty member can find a way to interest them. If called on to do so, faculty tend to justify the use of grades by defining them as some kind of combined measure of ability and interest. But some student actions make a mockery of that definition, being designed to produce the end product—grades—without an appropriate input of ability, interest, and effort.

Actions designed to circumvent the ability-effort equation, then, may be regarded as illegitimate. We have already noted that students attempt

---

[3] We made a practice of describing in detail the student rooms we visited and were thus able to check this point in our field notes.

to get information on instructors' prejudices and idiosyncrasies. They act on that information, and even act when they have no information and must rely on guesswork. They want to affect the instructor's judgment of their work and thus raise their grade, either by catering to his prejudices or by getting to know him personally and taking advantage of the personal acquaintance in some way.

The conception underlying such actions is embodied in the commonly used phrase "brownie points." The vulgar origins of the expression are quite lost on campus; innocent young girls use it freely. One gains brownie points, of course, by "brown-nosing," by doing things that will gain the instructor's favor other than simply doing the assigned classwork. The phrase is commonly used in a half-joking way, but its import is perfectly serious. One student explained the technique in detail (though he used a more refined term):

> What I do is apple-polishing, but it's not so obvious as that. It all depends on the teacher. Mainly, I just get to know them. I go up to their offices and talk with them. [What do you talk about?] Anything, anything they feel like talking about. I might figure out a good question to ask them. That'll show them that I'm really thinking about the course. And sometimes I just go up and say hello and we sit down and start talking about things. Maybe we'll talk about new cars. I'll say I don't like the new Ford this year, what do you think of it? And he'll tell me what he thinks of it.
>
> Just different problems like that. You know, these teachers don't like to talk about their subject all the time, they get tired of it, day in, day out, the same thing. I just size them up and see what I think they will go for. Now my English teacher last year, he was a tough one to figure out the second semester. It took me almost a whole semester to figure out what to do about him. Finally, I figured it out. I praised him, that's what he liked. It paid off, too. I got my mark raised a whole grade.
>
> *October, 1959, sophomore fraternity man*

One can get negative brownie points as well—lose points by doing something formally extraneous to the course work which irritates or annoys the instructor; he is thought to retaliate by lowering one's grade:

> Prentice said, "Boy, I've got minus brownie points in my speech class. I'm about 200 in the hole to her." His friend said, "What do you mean?" Prentice said, "Well, she just doesn't like me. She's got some reasons too. I mean, they're pretty good reasons." The observer said, "For instance?" Prentice said, "Well, for one thing, I didn't show up for an appointment with her, you know, it was supposed to be for my benefit. She was going to help me out. I just didn't show up, so that doesn't go over too good. And I haven't been to class in a long time."
>
> *May, 1960, freshman independent men*

Students fear, particularly, that disagreeing with the instructor, in class or in a paper, will have bad results:

> You can write a very good theme on some subject—I mean, the grammar can be perfect and the spelling and the punctuation and everything—and they'll flunk you, if you write something they don't agree with. I've seen it happen. They don't like for you to have a different interpretation than the one they think is right. You take a piece of poetry, for instance. They'll pretty much tell you what you should get out of it, how it should impress you. They'll ask you to write a theme about it. Well, you'd better get the same impressions from it that they told you you should have, or you're going to be in trouble. . . . It just doesn't pay to disagree with them, there's no point in it. The thing to do is find out what they want you to say and tell them that.
>
> *October, 1959, junior fraternity man*

(It is for this reason, of course, that students seek to discover the tastes and prejudices of the faculty in the ways described in the preceding chapter.)

Students also act illegitimately when they attempt to improve their grade by disputing the instructor's interpretation of a term paper or an examination question. As every faculty member knows, returning papers or exams often provokes spirited debate designed to demonstrate that the answer the teacher thought incorrect was really correct, that the paper he thought inadequate actually measured up to the requirements he had set. And, as every teacher also knows, a student can often raise his grade by such tactics; students are ingenious in discovering hidden ambiguities in examination questions and term paper assignments. Here is an example:

> I had to wring a C out of the psychology man [the instructor]. I had to argue with him, you should have seen me. The thing was, on that essay question he took off because I didn't give a name [a heading] for each point. There were eight points and I got each one in the discussion but I thought I would be different and just describe it and not give the name, so he counted off two points for each one, but I made him put some back and that gives me a C.
>
> *November, 1959, junior independent girl*

Arguments over the interpretation of an answer or assignment seem illegitimate to faculty because, again, they are ways of circumventing the equation of ability and effort with grades. They turn the grade into something that can be achieved by using the academically extraneous skills of a "Philadelphia lawyer."

Some students engage in the ultimate illegitimate act—cheating. A national survey of academic dishonesty among college students suggests, however, that students and faculty differ with respect to the definition of cheating.[4] Students seldom consider that they have cheated when they consult one another about an assignment. But faculty members, who see the teacher-student relationship as a one-to-one relationship between themselves and each individual student (a dyadic model of learning), sometimes feel that if the student consults anyone else he has acted dishonestly. By doing so, he has made his grade depend in some part on the ability and effort of others. (In view of the common scholarly practice of circulating work before publication for collegial comment and criticism, this faculty notion seems unduly rigorous.)

Some acts are on the borderline. A good many students might agree with faculty members that the following chemistry "shortcut" is illegitimate:

> They give you a sample of something and you're supposed to figure out what's in it. They only give you so much of it. The idea is if you use it all up making the wrong tests then you're just out of luck, you fail on that experiment. But guys are getting another sample out of them. You know, they say that their partner knocked the jar over or that they tripped while they are carrying it and spilled it or something like that. I've seen two fellows get away with it. So I don't think it'll be all that tough, if you can get around things like that.
>
> *October, 1959, sophomore fraternity man*

(But we should note that medical students regard similar shortcuts as essential and do not consider them cheating.[5])

The same national survey reveals that grosser forms of cheating are quite widespread. Fifty per cent of the students questioned admitted that they had, at least once during their college careers, copied during an examination, used crib notes, plagiarized published materials for a term paper, or turned in someone else's paper. We saw very little obvious cheating, although we saw many borderline actions. One case of copying on an examination came to our attention, and one theft of an examination from a departmental office occurred during the time we were in the field. Nevertheless, some cheating must have occurred that we did not see; the nature of the act and students' shame at engaging in it (also documented in the survey referred to) make it hard to detect.

The most important point about illegitimate actions is that they are a consequence of the existence of a system of examinations, grades, and grade point averages. If the faculty uses examinations and other assignments to evaluate the student's abilities or progress, some students will attempt to influence the outcome of the evaluation "illegally," by "brown-

4 William Bowers, *Student Dishonesty and Its Control in College* (New York: Bureau of Applied Social Research, Columbia University, 1964).
5 *Cf.* Becker et al., *op. cit.*, pp. 116–117 and 170–173.

nosing," arguing, or cheating. Illegitimate actions would be foolish if nothing important could be gained from them. It is because they may be rewarded by a raised grade that students engage in them.

The GPA and Lowered Student Effort. The grade point average perspective does not always intensify student academic effort. In fact, it can depress the level of effort a student puts forth, if he feels that he is already in such serious trouble that no conceivable amount of effort will get him out; when he sees his situation this way, he may stop working altogether. If we compare students to the industrial workers studied by Donald Roy, the analogy to a monetary system is again revealing. The workers Roy studied felt that they were "entitled" to a certain hourly average when they worked on piecework. If piecework rates were set so tightly that workers could not achieve the specified amount, they then worked at well below their capacity.[6] Since they could not "make out," they might as well simply collect their hourly wage and be done with it. They saw no sense in expending effort when nothing could be gained.

College students act much the same way. When they know they cannot possibly win, they resign themselves to losing and do not throw good money after bad. Failing students refuse even to calculate their grade point average; they know that they are going to fail and are not interested in the exact degree of failure:

> Brown said, "I sure am going to have to work and pull my grade average up if I want to stay here." The observer said, "What is it now?" He laughed and said, "I haven't even figured it out. It's too awful to think about." Carlson said, "I haven't either. I don't know what I'm going to get in some of these courses, but I know it's going to be pretty bad and I don't really want to bother figuring what my average is. What good would it do? I know I've got to bring everything up."
>
> *January, 1961, two independent men, freshman and sophomore*

Likewise, students who are so far behind that it seems impossible to catch up do not bother to do assigned work anymore and sometimes stop doing all schoolwork completely; they report (to the observers and to each other) that they are unable to muster the energy or spirit to do the work:

> Tucker said, "Well, you're a damn fool. You just don't even try." Long said, "Buddy, I just can't get my spirit up. I don't know what's the matter with me." Tucker said, "I know how you feel. I feel the same way. There just doesn't seem to be any point to studying. I mean, I don't feel that I can learn anything and if I did it wouldn't be worth it so the hell with it."
>
> *May, 1960, three independent men, a freshman, and two juniors*

[6] Donald Roy, "Quota Restriction and Goldbricking in a Machine Shop," *American Journal of Sociology*, 57 (March, 1952), pp. 427–442.

The importance students attach to grades is thus exhibited in reverse. If one has already done so poorly that nothing can be salvaged, there is no point in studying or working.

ORGANIZATIONAL ACTIONS

Student organizations (primarily living groups) also engage in actions designed to get higher grades for their members. They may attempt to produce optimal study conditions, so that individual students can put forth their best effort, or they may provide specific help to students who need it.

The necessity of organizational action arises from certain common features of campus living groups. First, students usually live together in large groups. Whether in the fraternity or sorority house, the dormitory, or some other setting, the presence of large numbers of students makes it difficult to find sufficient peace and quiet for effective study. Other students may make so much noise that one cannot concentrate; they may interrupt studying by coming into one's room to talk; they may provide a variety of tempting distractions. Consequently, student groups find it necessary to make rules that allow people to study without interference when they want to, and to create machinery to enforce those rules. (What the situation can be like in the absence of such controls can best be seen in the halls of a freshman dormitory early in the year. Students run up and down the halls shouting and making a great deal of noise, running in and out of one another's rooms, and so on. The noise is deafening, and it is difficult to believe that anyone could study under such conditions.)

Second, as we have seen, the collective GPA of a living group helps determine its campus prestige. Living groups with a good reputation wish to maintain it; those attempting to rise want to do something to improve their rank. In both cases, they must help those members whose academic weakness will lower the living-group average.

Some living groups, ordinarily the fraternities and sororities, can exert effective control over their members more easily than can others, and they are likely to have effective discipline and elaborate programs of self-help. Others have more makeshift arrangements.

Let us take a highly developed fraternity scholarship program as an example. The fraternity may engage, as a group and on behalf of its members, in all the activities that we have already described for individuals; in particular, they will make an effort to see that pledges, who must "make their grades" to be initiated, do not fail. The house scholarship chairman coordinates the activities; he may be assisted by many others, who give special aid to students in fields in which they are expert.

The scholarship chairman keeps a close watch on the GPA of each pledge as the semester progresses:

> We pay the salary of a graduate student. . . . He has a complete record of every pledge's grades so he knows just what each guy is doing every day. . . . The pledges have to report to him every time they get a grade on a paper or a test or something and he keeps their average all figured out.
>
> *January, 1961, junior fraternity man*

When signs of trouble appear, the scholarship chairman seeks information about the cause of the trouble:

> What we do is that if we find a guy is slipping on his grades we go over and see his professor and we find out that he's been cutting his classes or something like that, why we know what to do about it.
>
> *January, 1961, junior fraternity man*

And the fraternity takes action to see that students having trouble get the help they need:

> The other part of our program is that we try to help the students with some of the courses that are giving them trouble so that they will have a better chance of passing. In other words, we try to give them help in studying for the course and in learning how to pass examinations. . . . It more or less amounts to a tutoring system. We have actives in the house who are particularly good in one subject or another that the freshmen take. . . . For instance, in chemistry we have a fellow who is majoring in chemistry who is very good in Chem I and Chem II particularly, so he will have review sessions with the boys that are taking that course. What he'll do is go over it, go over the material and ask them some questions and see what areas they're weak in and then he'll drill them on those areas. Of course, he's very sharp on what kinds of questions they'll ask on the examinations so he will give them problems to do that are very much like the problems they'll get on the examinations and that's a big help. The same thing with English. We've got a couple of fellows who are very good in English and they will help the pledges with their themes, help them with their sentence construction and choice of words and things of that kind.
>
> *January, 1961, junior fraternity man*

The help given freshmen by their older fraternity brothers sometimes verges on the "illegal," as may be the case in the following instance. We have no idea how frequently fraternity men overextend themselves on behalf of pledges.

> The scholarship chairman said that he didn't have all the grades in for the pledges but that three of them had gotten F's in English. The president of the fraternity asked, "What's the matter with them?" The scholarship chairman said, "I haven't had time to go into it yet." The president said, "Well,

maybe I'd better run upstairs and write that theme for Jones." Then he looked at me and acted as though he had said something very wrong, and said, "I mean, *help* him with his theme." I said, "Go ahead and write it for him. I won't tell anybody." The president said, "As a matter of fact, we tried that once and it doesn't work very well."

January, 1961, junior fraternity man

The most striking aspect of the way fraternities (those with less elaborate scholarship programs as well) handle academic problems, however, is the required study hall, explained this way by a scholarship chairman:

In the evening it simply means that between certain hours the pledges have to be in their rooms and they should be studying. Of course, there's an active [member] in the room with each pledge and if the active is reading a book, why the pledge is very likely to be studying too. We haven't really had any trouble with that at all. During the day we have a study hall over on the hill [the campus]. . . . It's in Watson Library. What it is is we have one of the actives up in the library to act as a proctor. He knows which pledges are supposed to be in the library at what hours and he stays there and makes sure they show up and that when they are there they study. In other words, he sees to it that they don't spend their time horsing around or sleeping, because you will see a lot of guys sleeping up there in Watson Library.

January, 1961, junior fraternity man

The effectiveness of the discipline imposed by fraternity study rules is startling. One observer went to dinner at a fraternity house and spent half an hour after dinner in casual conversation with some of the members. He noted many people going to and fro. Suddenly, at seven o'clock (when study hall began), he found himself alone in the living room of the fraternity house. Every student in the house had gone to his room to study.

Opinions about the effectiveness of required study differ. Some scholarship chairmen feel that it provokes anger among the pledges and that, once they have been initiated, students who were subjected to study hall are likely to backslide. Some have noticed, in addition, that brighter students, who study without being coerced, may find the requirement galling. In at least one case known to us, a bright student depledged his fraternity, in part over this issue.

Student groups that do not have the organizational means of achieving such elaborate discipline often attempt it anyway. Several times we saw dormitory wings or floors make elaborate rules designed to improve studying conditions. They might, for instance, forbid running or loud talking in the corridors between seven and ten in the evening or fix hours during which hi-fi equipment could not be played. But the absence of effective enforcement meant that these rules worked only as long as the goodwill and motivation of everyone lasted. Ordinarily, dormitory discipline was lax and studying was frequently difficult. (Both fraternity men and dormitory dwellers, however, could use the library and empty classrooms as quiet places in which to study without interruption in the evening.)

Students in less well-organized living groups also try to provide each other with help in studying, though with less success. The actions of a great many people must be organized and coordinated, and fraternities and sororities are better equipped for the job. Independents, therefore, usually study in two-, three-, and four-man partnerships, in the hope that several heads will be better than one. We often observed scenes like the following, both in the dormitories and in student hangouts:

> Two girls had come in to study with a boy. They opened up their books and began to study biology. They would ask each other questions in a very formal way as if they were taking a quiz, and then busily thumb through the textbooks and write in their notebooks. I could not see whether they were reviewing old exams or not.
>
> *January, 1961, three independents, two freshman girls, and a freshman man*

Similarly, a large dormitory (or a scholarship hall which, though smaller, has a high percentage of good students) can often give effective help to the student with academic problems. If he can find a person who knows something about the subject he needs help with and can prevail on the "expert" to give his time (which students usually are willing to do for one another), he may get very effective aid. But the search is left to his own initiative and knowledge of the strengths of others, instead of being formally arranged, and many students lack one or the other requisite.

Various informal arrangements help students to protect themselves from their own temptation not to study. The following remarks, made by a freshman in danger of failing, illustrate one such arrangement:

> See, I wasn't used to sitting down and actually working. You know what I mean? I'd goof off too much. So I told all the other guys on the wing, "If I come into your room and I want to talk or bullshit or something like that, ask me first did I finish all my assignments for tomorrow. If I haven't finished all my assignments, kick my ass out." And they've been real good. They don't let me come in their room unless I tell them I finished all my work. And I don't tell them no lies.
>
> *October, 1960, freshman independent man*

Students sometimes, although rarely, attempt to "restrict production": to put pressure on others to keep the collective level of effort down so that others in the group will not have difficulty. Collective control of effort has been commonly reported in industry, and has also been observed in a medical school and in the freshman year at the Harvard Business School.[7] It appears to play a much smaller role in the college. Restriction of production probably occurs infrequently because, in contrast to the situations just mentioned, the classroom group (the equivalent of the industrial work group) has little opportunity for interaction and the building of consensus. The effective student group is the living group; but living-group members seldom find themselves together in class, and no class is made up exclusively of members of one living group. Members of the same class, as we have already noted, may have little in common, for college students are scattered through a great many courses with different instructors and seldom have as many as two of their classes together. There is little opportunity for a stable group to grow up, all of whom face the same problems in the same situation (as is the case in the schools and industries mentioned).

We did, however, hear occasional references, for instance, to "damned average-raisers," to those students who made such high grades on examinations that they raised the class average and made it difficult for other students to get good grades. We occasionally heard students tell others who were doing well in their classes to stop studying so much; though this was usually said in a joking way, it may have conveyed a more serious message. And we sometimes heard students complain bitterly about actions of others that had created additional academic difficulties for them:

> We have really got it in for that guy Thompson. It's because of him that we're going to have a second examination in Insurance. We weren't going to have one but that Thompson didn't do very well on the first one. He only got 78. I got 82 or 83, I can't remember. Anyway, he went around and told the professor that we would like to have another exam. Actually, all he wants to do is have another chance to raise his grade. As far as I'm concerned, it's just another chance to bring my grade down. I'd be glad to settle for what I have. I don't know what we're going to do with him, but we're going to do something. What I'd like to do is make sure that he doesn't make it to that exam and then he won't get anything for it and that would serve him right.
>
> *May, 1961, independent senior man*

[7] Roy, *ibid.;* Becker et al., *op. cit.;* and Charles D. Orth 3rd, *Social Structure and Learning Climate: The First Year at the Harvard Business School* (Boston: Graduate School of Business Administration, Harvard University, 1963).

CHAPTER **8**

BASES OF JUDGMENT
AND EVALUATION

Participants in organizations often have occasion to discriminate among the occupants of the various social positions with whom they regularly interact. They may, for instance, have the opportunity to choose one or a few among the many occupants of a given position as the ones with whom they will personally establish some kind of relationship. Thus patients often have the chance to decide which of the many available physicians they would like to have treat them; and people can often select from a large number of fellow workers those with whom they would like to become friendly. To make these discriminations and selections, participants in the organization use a system of evaluation, some standard of judgment that can be applied to specific cases.

Even when participants cannot choose whom they will interact with, they may still use a standard of judgment to decide what kind of person they are dealing with and what the best way of acting toward him is. When one has a doctor bureaucratically assigned to him, he still wants to know what kind of a person that doctor is and how his words and actions are to be interpreted.[1]

In the same way, participants in organizations often have occasion to assess themselves. They may want to know how they compare as participants, asking: "How good am I?" "How do I compare with others in a similar position in the organization?" They may use the answers to decide, for example, whether they ought to continue as participants or perhaps move elsewhere. They may also ask such questions in a more profound way, using the answers to questions about organizational perfor-

[1] See Julius A. Roth, *Timetables* (Indianapolis: The Bobbs-Merrill Co., 1963), *passim*.

108

mance as indicators of more general traits and thus arriving at some measure of their overall personal worth. In either case, they again use a standard of judgment.

Standards of judgment can, of course, be private and idiosyncratic, and such standards are often used, even in the most highly organized environments. But we can also expect that, under specific conditions that we might discover by comparative organizational analysis, standards of judgment will be incorporated as well into the perspective of the group. In the first place, if judgments must be made collectively or must be justified to other members of the organization, a common standard will facilitate matters. In addition, if the structure and practices of the organization subject participants to essentially similar treatment, they will probably be disposed to make use in a similar way of their common experience.

We can expect, then, that an important part of any perspective will be a set of criteria by which other participants and oneself can be judged. While not every perspective will contain such a standard, the presence of a standard in which the central themes of the perspective are taken as criteria of judgment may be interpreted as evidence of the dominance and ubiquity of the perspective.

In the college, we can see evidence of a standard related to the grade point average perspective in two areas. First, we may note the general principle that whenever two categories of people have to cooperate in some common enterprise, one is likely to judge the other by how much or how little he contributes to the success of the enterprise as one has defined it. Thus workers in service occupations tend to judge their clients or customers by how easy they make it for the worker to achieve his occupational goals. Teachers prefer pupils who learn quickly.[2] Musicians prefer an audience that lets them play as they wish, without interference.[3]

Students make assessments of this kind about faculty members, judging them according to how difficult the faculty member makes it for them, through various actions he takes, to achieve what they want to achieve in class. We conclude that the grade point average perspective is a dominant influence on the way students approach their academic work in part because we observe that major criterion students use in evaluating faculty members is how difficult they make it for the student to achieve his own version of academic success.

[2] Howard S. Becker, "Social Class Variations in the Teacher-Pupil Relationship," *Journal of Educational Sociology,* 25 (April, 1952), pp. 451–465.
[3] Howard S. Becker, *Outsiders: Studies in the Sociology of Deviance* (New York: The Free Press, 1963), Chapters 5 and 6.

Organizational participants also evaluate themselves and other occupants of their own position in the organization. Insofar as certain things are defined by the organization's rules as valuable and worthwhile (and the definition is accepted by participants), one can judge oneself and one's peers by how much of that valuable thing they accumulate, particularly when the valuable involved is congruent with the actors' generalized goals. In a money economy people tend to judge their own and each other's worth by the amount of money they accumulate.

Students make their judgments of themselves and one another in this way. They take the chief valuable institutionalized by the college and reinforced by the living group prestige system—grades—and use it as a way of making personal judgments. Grades reflect a person's worth; inadequate grades indicate an important personal deficiency.

Grades are a particularly apt basis of judgment because they can be connected with the generalized goal of achieving maturity while in college. Students reason that one is doing well in his academic work if he achieves the academic rewards the college offers; doing well indicates maturity. Likewise, the inability to get the grades one wants means, in their eyes, that one is not quite grown up. In short, they accept the University system as it is expressed in the rules.

We have counted as evidence of the existence of the grade point average perspective all those incidents in which students base their evaluation of someone on the criterion of grades.

STUDENT JUDGMENTS OF FACULTY

Students feel they must do their academic work in such a way as to earn a grade that will be satisfactory for them. Grades are awarded by the faculty and can be earned only by pleasing the faculty. It is not surprising that students find faculty behavior, particularly in reference to grades and associated matters, of great concern. Nor is it surprising that students make judgments of individual faculty members. Of the various bases on which students might make those judgments, the importance of the grading system imposed by faculty and administration suggests that they will use the effect of the professor's actions on their grades as one important criterion. It is not just the professor's grading practices that are the issue, but all of his actions that influence the pursuit of grades. The amount of work he assigns, the clarity of his assignments, and a host of similar matters make it easier or more difficult to meet his requirements adequately, and student judgments based on these points thus reflect the GPA perspective.

Students make judgments of faculty members that reflect their conception of how a faculty member ought to behave. Since the judgments most often take the form of complaints, our analysis will be concerned mainly with the kinds of complaints students make about faculty members and the conception of proper faculty behavior that underlies them. This does not mean that students do nothing but complain about their instructors, nor does it mean that they think most instructors are bad. We focus on complaints because when things go well and people (in this case, professors) behave as they ought to, students do not ordinarily remark on it; but when expectations are violated, complaints emerge and can be used to understand the expectations that are ordinarily met.

Students' complaints, then, register the various ways a professor may fail to live up to students' conceptions of how he ought to behave so that they can get acceptable grades. One might say, if it did not make the matter sound more conscious and formal than it is, that students have adopted a code of fair play and expect the faculty to follow it. When faculty members break the code, students complain. They may complain because they cannot find out what the rules of the course are, because the teacher assigns more work than they can comfortably handle, given their other commitments, or because they think the grading system unfair.

Students do not judge faculty members solely on these bases. As we shall see when we consider negative cases in the next chapter, they sometimes discriminate between professors who are interesting and those who are not. In addition, they sometimes praise a professor for "really knowing his subject." They sometimes object to professors who are poorly dressed or have irritating personal mannerisms. But these reactions occur rarely and, furthermore, are unrelated to any larger set of student interests in the way concern over the effect of the professor's actions on academic achievement is.

Nor do students choose their instructors according to the GPA perspective, though, all other things being equal, they prefer those who stand well on this criterion to those who do not. (But they do not have much choice of instructor anyway, because of the restrictions on their choice of courses and the way instructors are assigned in multisection courses; also, they do, of course, make use of other criteria in evaluating instructors.)

Giving Information. Students prefer professors who give unambiguous instructions about what will be required and clear indications of what materials they will be held responsible for knowing if they are to get a good grade. They complain when the instructor's style of teaching does not give sufficient cues to enable them to tell what he wants them to learn. A common complaint is: "I can't take notes on his lectures." The complaint rests on the student assumption that a "good teacher" will make clear which points are major and must be remembered, which are only illustrations that need not be bothered with, and what the logical order of the points made is. An instructor who lectures in this fashion gives the students material for notes that are easy to study for examinations; one who does not intensifies the student's academic problems:

> Now you see, here I am trying to take decent well-outlined notes and this guy comes along and does that. You just put down that this will be discussed later like he said, and then right away he starts discussing it. Your notes are all messy, you can't keep them straight that way. . . . He's a lousy teacher, all right. . . . You never know what to study for class and I don't know how I'll be able to tell what to study for examinations.
>
> *October, 1959, fraternity junior*

Amount of Work Given. Professors are not ordinarily aware of the many demands made on the student's time; they seldom know what he has to do in anyone else's classroom. They know even less, of course, about a student's nonacademic involvements, activities, and ambitions. They do not, ordinarily, know what organizations he belongs to or what offices he holds; they do not know the demands these make on his time and effort. Nor do they know the state of his social life; if he has a girl friend who complains that she never sees him because he is always studying, few of his instructors will be aware of this. And, finally, few faculty members would take seriously the student idea that a mature and successful student will apportion his time among all these things wisely; they are more likely to believe that organizational activities and personal relationships are entitled only to the time and energy left after a maximum academic effort has been made.

It would, of course, be unreasonable to expect instructors to know the amount and timing of all their students' work obligations; each student has somewhat different responsibilities because he has different courses and different instructors, varying considerably in what they require.[4] It would be utopian to expect them to have knowledge of students' nonacademic commitments. And that, perhaps, would not be such a good idea anyway; students deserve a certain amount of privacy. A student may take as few as fourteen hours of courses a week or as

---

[4] It would not be unreasonable, however, to suggest that this might be a proper faculty concern and that faculties might arrange to have simple research done that would give them some notion of what obligations their students actually have. For example, one might do a sample census of students, asking them to list the number of hours they actually spend in the classroom or laboratory, the amount of reading required and recommended, the number and kind of examinations given, and the timing of all these obligations. It is our guess that the results of such a survey would come as a great surprise to most faculty members who, in our experience, tend to underestimate the amount of work students do and must do.

many as twenty. But these figures, even if the instructor had them available for his students, do not give a true or sufficiently detailed picture. A laboratory course, for instance, may be listed as a four-hour-a-week course, but actually require the student's presence in the lab for many more hours. More importantly, the mere number of hours a week gives no clue as to the immense variety in amount and kind of work required.

Some classes require a steady and consistent input of relatively small amounts of effort, some form of daily "homework," be it solving math problems, preparing short themes, or getting ready for short weekly exams. Others require periodic investments of more sizable amounts of effort: a midterm exam, a paper, and a final exam, for instance. (In the latter case, of course, the student could also put forth a small consistent effort; but the tendency is to take advantage of the possibility of doing otherwise.) Some courses require a large amount of reading; others require fuller mastery of a smaller body of material. The student must allocate his time so as to meet all these requirements successfully, where their number, difficulty, and scheduling make that possible.

Because the demands of different instructors in different kinds of courses are nowhere coordinated, the student will sometimes find the burden of assignments from his several courses more than he can comfortably manage in the time at his disposal. When this occurs he tends to blame the faculty for requiring too much effort for the contribution the grade will make to the GPA (even though the problem arises, as it may, from his own inability to schedule his work rationally):

> It's only fifteen hours [of courses], but it's an awful lot of work. They expect you to do as much reading for the two-hour course as for the three-hour course and they expect you to do a hell of a lot of reading for the three-hour course.
>
> *October, 1960, senior independent man*

The sheer amount of work may not upset students so much as the way it is scheduled. Examinations, due dates for term papers, and other assignments all seem to run together (largely because the University requires midterm reports on student progress), so that the student finds he has a great deal of work to do in a very short time. The faculty, by ignoring the piling-up of assignments, makes it difficult for the student to do what he must for his grades:

> You know, I've got the funniest kind of cycle going in my school work. It's really not too good. I have nothing at all to do for about three weeks except loaf along and then it seems like every fourth week I'm just swamped with papers, tests, and so on. It's like that in every class. They all seem to come out together. [The interviewer said, "It seems to me that a wise man would

look ahead and get some of it done early."] No, you can't do that. You know that you're going to have a paper to write the fourth week but they don't tell you what it's about until the beginning of that week so there's nothing to do but wait for it.

October, 1960, sophomore independent man

Paradoxically, some students complain if there are too few assignments. The teacher uses the results of each assignment in calculating the final grade. The fewer assignments, the more each will count in the final grade and the more dangerous it is to do poorly on one; as the number of assignments grows, each one becomes less important, and the student has many more chances to make up for a poor showing. A student complained, at the beginning of a course:

> He really made it sound like we're going to have to work our balls off in there. You know what he said? He said that there are only going to be two examinations, one midterm and one final [and a term paper] . . . . Three measly things, that's all you've got to make your grade out of. If you fuck up on one of them you're screwed. That's no good. I like it where there are more little assignments and you've got a chance to make up for any bad mistakes you make.

February, 1960, sophmore independent man

Grading Procedures. Because they think grades so important, students want them to be awarded in a way that is both fair and serious. To return to our monetary analogy, it is as though they wanted to be paid a fair wage for their work, in currency that has real value recognized by others in the community, and paid according to some impersonal set of rules, rather than being subject to an employer's arbitrary whims. When a professor violates any of these expectations, students complain.[5]

They complain most of arbitrariness or random variation in grades, of methods of assigning grades based on anything other than the worth of the student's work.[6] For instance, some professors are reputed never to give high grades, no matter how good a student's work is:

> I seem to have had the misfortune to take a history class with a man who just doesn't believe in giving A's. I know this graduate student who had taken three courses from him and never managed to get an A yet. . . . We seem to have a disagreement because I've written two examination papers that I thought were good A papers and he thought were good B papers.

December, 1960, sophomore independent man

[5] Howard S. Becker, Blanche Geer, Everett C. Hughes, and Anselm L. Strauss, *Boys in White: Student Culture in Medical School* (Chicago: University of Chicago Press, 1961), pp. 121–24.
[6] See the interesting parallel in Carl Werthman, "Delinquents in Schools: A Test for the Legitimacy of Authority," *Berkeley Journal of Sociology*, 8 (1963), pp. 39–60.

Students complain, too, that the value of a grade varies from course to course in a more or less random way, so that a person's GPA may reflect neither his ability nor the amount of effort he has expended but rather the courses he took or the chance by which he was assigned to any easy- or hard-grading instructor. They reason that although those who use grades as a criterion for judging students could in theory make allowance for difficult courses or difficult professors, in practice a low grade lowers the average and those who assess the student on the basis of his average (admissions committees of professional or graduate schools, for instance) will not know about or make allowance for these special circumstances:

> There's one bad thing about the university. The grading. It simply isn't consistent from one class to another. The A's you can get from one teacher may not be any better than a C from another teacher. Some teachers mark on a curve and others don't. I mean, you don't know where you stand.
>
> *February, 1960, fraternity senior*

Students decide that grades vary randomly, without reference to student ability, when grade point averages of students they know do not jibe with their own assessment of those students' ability:

> I got a 2.7 average, but you know what burns me up? There's a girl from my home town who I know who got a 3.0 average. . . . She never got a 3.0 average the whole time she was in high school. She just isn't that smart, that's all. . . . She studies a lot and she gets all that stuff into her head but she's not really that smart.
>
> *February, 1960, freshman independent man*

Many administrative and pedagogic procedures strike students as "unfair" because they result in inequities in grading. Instructors teaching different sections of the same course may use different techniques, some of which are (no matter what their educational virtues) poorer preparation for the final examination than others. The method of calculating the GPA, to take another example, seems unfair to some students: a B that is almost an A and a B that is almost a C count equally; if course grades were given in decimals, the overall GPA would reflect the student's achievement more accurately.

Although students ordinarily attribute inequities in grading to a lack of coordination among professors or to professorial idiosyncrasy, they sometimes suspect the instructor of acting in ways that devalue the grading system entirely. To the student, grades are a serious matter. He may not approve of particular grading practices, he may find that the grading system makes things difficult for him, but he still believes that grades are, in general, an appropriate and adequate measure of a student's academic work. When a professor, for some extraneous reason, gives a student a higher grade than he deserves, the student may congratulate himself on his luck but may also respond with anger, because the very act by which he profits also serves to devalue all grades. If one student can get a grade he did not deserve, any student might do so. If this should happen on any large scale, the grading system would be worthless as a measure of student worth. That students respond to what they perceive as a perversion of the grading system with anger indicates the seriousness with which they view grades. In one case reported in our field notes the fieldworker asked a well-known campus athlete, "Listen, tell me something, do all of your professors know who you are?" The student understood the question immediately and said:

> Well, yes, I guess they do. That's something that sort of bothers me sometimes because I'm not just sure about my grades. Like I had one course and out of one hundred points I got only nineteen and I ended up with a B for the course. Now, I don't know, but I think that the professors all know that I have to be out practicing and I think they take that into account.
>
> *October, 1960, fraternity senior*

On another occasion, a student who held high political office on campus said:

> One thing around here, I wonder why grades have to be so subjective. There's a faculty member that I got on a committee he wanted to be on and I had three papers that were graded C, and after that he gave me six hours of A's.
>
> *July, 1959, fraternity senior*

Students, in short, do not want to be paid in worthless currency.

JUDGMENTS OF OTHER STUDENTS AND ONESELF

Students have occasion, for a variety of personal and institutional reasons, to make discriminations among their fellow students. They have to choose new members for fraternities and sororities, officers and jobholders for campus organizations, friends, persons to date, and so on. To make these choices, they require a criterion on which to base them.

Students also evaluate themselves. Given their generalized goal of becoming more mature while they are in college, they construct situationally specific perspectives that define maturity as doing well in the several areas of campus life, of which the academic area is one. They use conventional benchmarks to judge how well they are approaching maturity; to construct those benchmarks they use a criterion that furnishes the dimension along which their progress can be gauged. Grades provide the criterion.

Grades are likely to be used as a basis of judgment of the personal worth of other students and oneself for several reasons. In spite of their obvious deficiencies (many of which were mentioned in the preceding section), they are both impersonal and available for every student on campus; other bases of judgment are likely to be subjective and to be available for only some students or for only those students whom the evaluator knows personally. By using grades as a criterion, one can rank oneself and other students in comparison with the entire campus.

In addition, grades seem to students a particularly apt and reliable measure of character and maturity. Earning satisfactory grades is like earning a living, a sign of steadiness, of ability to discipline oneself and stick to the job. Conversely, a person who cannot "make his grades" must, like a person who cannot earn a living, have something wrong with him; there must be some reason for his failure and, whatever it is, it cannot speak well of him. This is particularly so since students think that it is not difficult to get adequate grades, if one is willing to apply oneself as much as necessary:

> I think anybody could get through college by doing just a little work. I think if you worked an hour for every subject for every day you could get B's, or anyway C's. I really think anyone could get through with a D who worked about an hour and a half a night. I work about an hour on some subjects and others take me only fifteen minutes. Then there are other courses that anyone could understand if they just took the trouble to do the reading.
>
> *November, 1959, freshman independent girl*

Obviously, a person who will not take even this small amount of trouble cannot be thought mature; he has failed in his main task at college, at least in this area of college life.

We have seen that judgments based on the grade point average are incorporated into the bylaws governing student organizations. Fraternities, sororities, and campus organizations all have mandatory minimal GPA requirements, without which the student cannot become a member or an officer. In addition, many organizations require higher averages than the minimum requirements. In this section we consider not these institutionally embodied judgments, but the more personal and intimate judgments made in informal relationships.

Judgments of Oneself. Students use their own GPA to measure their progress toward the maturity they have come to college to achieve, as a way of making the most profound and personal judgments about themselves. A student who comes to college hopes and expects to do well; he thinks of himself as the kind of person who can master the problems college will pose for him. When he fails in his academic work, he is forced to recognize that he is not that kind of person; it is a bitter truth, and students try to evade it. As one failing student said, "What the hell! I can do it. I'm not a dumbbell." It is precisely the equation of getting failing grades and being a dumbbell or any of the several other bad things a failing student might be that is the point.

When a student gets low grades, he becomes very depressed by the realization that he is not as good as he thought he was; conversely, when he improves his grades, his outlook brightens:

> I failed everything [the semester before]. It was terrible. You know, that's an awful feeling. I mean, you can't think about anything else but just your homework and trying to get through and keep in school. And I couldn't think about going to any meetings or politics or anything. . . . I just decided to go to law school this semester, after I found out how well I did. You know, then you can start planning ahead. The other way, gee! I didn't even know if I would ever finish school or not.
>
> *March, 1961, independent sophomore man*

Students who are not failing, even students who are doing quite well, use grades to judge themselves too. They simply shift the cutting point up; a B or C, which might give a poorer student cause to think he was not such a bad fellow after all, reveals to them that they are not as serious and mature as they thought:

> But the way I feel about it is, the only grades that count are A's and B's. The whole range from minus one to 2.0 doesn't mean anything to me. . . . I figure if I can't do well enough in a course to get an A or a B, something is the matter with me.
>
> *March, 1961, fraternity junior*

Bright students find their schoolwork easy, and this makes them wonder whether their high grades really reflect the maturity they seek; perhaps, they think, they should set themselves more difficult tasks, such as taking a heavier course load:

> It doesn't seem any harder than junior college. In fact, I was kind of disappointed. Some of the courses actually seem easier. . . . It only adds up to seventeen hours of courses. . . . It's not as heavy a load as I thought I would carry when I came up here. I'm kind of disappointed in myself about that.
>
> *October, 1959, independent junior girl*

Bright students set themselves more difficult assignments than those given by the instructor, so that they may continue to use grades as a basis of self-judgment. They may undertake a larger piece of work than is called for. Or, as in the following incident, they may do a simple assignment in a humorous style, taking the risk of offending the instructor, but trusting to their ingenuity and wit to carry it off:

> I couldn't see any point in writing the kind of themes that kids usually write. You know how they go. I could have written one that would be like this: "My hometown is Prairieville. Prairieville has a lot of nice people in it. Prairieville is a medium-sized town. Prairieville. . . ." Well, I just couldn't see writing a paper like that so when he asked us to write about our home I started out by saying, "Home is where I hang my pool cue." And then I went on to describe pool halls I had spent a lot of time in. I got a good grade on that too. I mean, you can do those things and they're a lot more fun than doing it the regular way which would be too boring.
>
> *April, 1960, junior independent man*

Judgments of Others. Students, when they describe another student, frequently mention his grade point average as one of the important facts anyone would necessarily want to know. The statement of the person's average often either contains directly or implies an evaluation, negative if the average is low, positive if it is high. Thus a freshman pointed out an older fraternity brother to the observer and said, "You see him? He's got a 3.0 average in engineering. That's really something." Another student explained the rationale of using grades as a measure of personal worth and how a well-known campus leader's grades had affected his reputation:

> Until we get a better way of measuring, and we sure haven't got one now, why grades are the best way of measuring whether somebody is delivering. I think most students feel that way about it. They look on grades as a way of saying something about a guy. . . . Students are not going to have as much respect for somebody who doesn't get at least a 1.5. Now John [a campus political leader], I don't suppose his final average was anywhere near 1.5. It was closer to a 1.0. . . . It wasn't that anybody had it in for him because his grades weren't higher, but there were some things that they wouldn't have said about him if he'd put in a little more time studying.
>
> *March, 1961, senior fraternity man*

The criterion is even used in cross-sex references, where one might expect other criteria to be more important:

> That boy is going to flunk out. You can see why I won't go out with him. I don't want to go out with a boy who might be flunking out.
>
> *November, 1959, sorority sophomore*

The girl is doing more than making a judgment of the boy's maturity and personal worth. She is also recognizing that a boy who may have to leave the university will not be able to play the appropriate role in her social life; he will not be able to invite her to parties and will be less available for her to invite to her sorority's important formal social events, events for which she must have a date.

Knowing that a low GPA will cause others to think badly of them, students with low grades often try to keep their failure a secret. In the following incident, the observer must use forceful techniques to pry the truth out of a failing student:

> I said, "How did you make out last semester?" Jack looked a little shame-faced and said, "You mean grades?" I said, "Yeah." He said, "Not too good. Not too good at all, but I'm working a lot harder this semester." I said, "What do you mean, not too good?" I was determined to find out what he really meant. He said, "Well, it was pretty bad, to tell you the truth." I said, "Come on, Jack, don't be coy." He said, "Well, I'll tell you. I failed more courses than I passed." I said, "You mean you had a minus grade-point average?" He said, "That's right."
>
> *March, 1960, freshman independent man*

Students do not respect someone who achieves a high GPA by taking easy ("pud") courses, for it then does not testify to his maturity. Others must know that one's high grades were honestly come by. One student explained his choice of a double major on these grounds:

> Anthropology has that reputation of being an easy major, you know, the kind of thing you take because you have to have a major. I think really that's part of the reason I want to take a major in mathematics too, because everybody says, "Oh, well, anthropology, it's just a bunch of pud courses." It's not true, but it's hard to convince everybody of. So if they say that to me I can say, "Well, I'm also majoring in math." And no one thinks that those are pud courses.
>
> *March, 1960, freshman independent man*

This may seem paradoxical, for we know that students feel they must do whatever is necessary to get good grades; why not take as many "pud" courses as you can work into your schedule? The paradox is only apparent; the argument confuses two aspects of the perspective. On the one hand, students feel it necessary to get good grades and will, in pursuit of them, take "pud" courses if that seems the most likely way to achieve them. On the other hand, good grades are a sign of personal worth, but only because they indicate that their recipient has earned them by being maturely disciplined and hardworking. To get good grades in a way that does not demand mature behavior brings one no honor, and in this context "pud" courses, however expedient they may be, are held in disrespect.

CHAPTER 9

EVIDENCE FOR THE EXISTENCE
OF THE GRADE POINT AVERAGE
PERSPECTIVE

The perspective we have described is the one ordinarily used by students in dealing with the problems posed for them by the academic part of campus life. Let us be clear (at the risk of being repetitious) about what we mean. We do not mean that all students use the perspective at all times or that all students invariably undertake the actions we have described, or that students never have any other motive than getting good grades. We particularly do not mean that the perspective is the only possible way for students to deal with the academic side of campus life.

We do mean that the organization of campus life poses particular problems for students, growing out of the institutionalization of grades as the chief valuable in the area of academic work. As students, over the years, have dealt with those problems, they have developed collectively ways of thinking about them and ways of acting with respect to them that are coherent and workable. That is, their perspective hangs together in a more or less logical way and provides a means of dealing with academic problems that is more often successful than not. It might, given another history, have developed quite differently.

Because the chief characteristic of the organization in which the perspective is found is the *institutionalization* of grades as valuable, the chief characteristic of the perspective itself is the recognition that this is so and that student action must be oriented to this fact of life. The more specific details of the perspective arise out of the particular form the institutionalization of grades takes on this campus; we would not expect all campuses to be like the one we describe. And, on a campus where something other than grades was the major institutionalized form of value, we would not expect the GPA perspective to exist at all.

The evidence that the GPA perspective is ordinarily used by students in meeting academic problems consists of items from our field notes —conversations, descriptions of actions, and the like—which take one or more of the forms described in the preceding chapters. Any item having one or more of the characteristics we have described indicates the existence and use by students of the perspective. Our evidence shows that the perspective's use is frequent and widespread and, furthermore, that it is collective in character, shared by students and not developed by each student individually.

Evidence that use of the perspective is frequent is found in Tables 7

TABLE 7
Items of Evidence for the GPA Perspective

	Volunteered	Directed	Total
Statements			
Alone	562	9	571
Group	300	1	301
Activities			
Individual	62	—	62
Group	107	—	107
Total	1031	10	1041

and 8. Our field notes yielded a total of 1041 items indicating student use of the GPA perspective. It is hardly credible that a perspective that appeared infrequently on campus would appear so many times in our field notes, particularly since only ten items were directed by the observer

TABLE 8
Items of Evidence for the GPA Perspective,
by Category [a]

Definition of the situation	252
Seeking information and knowing GPA	217
Individual and collective actions	362
GPA as basis for judgment	210
Total	1041

[a] The categories are those covered in preceding chapters: definition, Chapters 4 and 5; information, Chapter 6; actions, Chapter 7; and judgment, Chapter 8.

(i.e., the observer introduced the element that made the item an instance of the perspective into the interaction, the student merely indicating assent).[1]

However, this conclusion must be evaluated in two ways. First, the number of items is obviously a function of the number of man-hours spent in the field. One might discover a thousand instances of anything on a college campus if he waited long enough. Is our finding simply the consequence of waiting long enough? There is, unfortunately, no simple test to use in making this judgment. Three observers were in the field, off and on, for two school years. The reader must interpret these figures for himself, keeping in mind the character of instances as these have been illustrated. In our own view, it is a very large number, and we consider the null hypothesis—that use of the perspective was not frequent—untenable.

The second way of evaluating the frequency of items that exhibit characteristics of the perspective is in relation to the number of negative items, items in which students make use of some alternative perspective. Using a generous criterion, we find seventy-six negative items, 6.8 per cent of the total number of items, positive and negative (1117). This small number of negative instances indicates that there were no seriously competing perspectives among the majority of the students. (We consider the character of the negative instances in some detail below.)

Use of the perspective was widespread as well. Items giving evidence of its use were gathered from men and women, from fraternity and sorority members as well as independents, from dormitory dwellers and rooming house residents, from students who were doing well academically and those who were not, from leaders of campus organizations as well as ordinary members and nonmembers, from Protestants, Catholics, and Jews, Negroes and whites, Kansans and non-Kansans, rural, small-town and city dwellers, and from students of various social classes. Items were gathered at all times of the year and in relation to a wide variety of courses, departments, and professors. In short, the evidence will not support any contention that the perspective was limited to any of the groups or situations listed.[2]

---

[1] For a fuller explanation of this method of evaluating field work evidence, see Howard S. Becker and Blanche Geer, "Participant Observation: The Analysis of Qualitative Data," in Richard N. Adams and Jack J. Preiss, eds., *Human Organization Research: Field Relations and Techniques* (Homewood, Ill.: The Dorsey Press, 1960), pp. 267–289; for an example of its use, see Howard S. Becker et al., *Boys in White: Student Culture in Medical School* (Chicago: University of Chicago Press, 1961), *passim.*

[2] A count of the relative frequency of items from students belonging to one or another of these categories would not be meaningful, because our hours in the field were not systematically distributed between the subdivisions of a category; nor could they have

Use of the perspective was collective, shared among the students as something that "everyone knows." Two characteristics of our evidence lead to this conclusion. First, as we have already noted, all but ten of the items discovered in our field notes were volunteered by students rather than being directed by the observer. This indicates that students were accustomed to use the perspective as part of their ordinary repertoire of strategies for dealing with the academic side of the campus.

Second, and more important, a substantial number of items consist of incidents in which students were observed using some aspect of the perspective in common, in which it furnished the basis for collective action or the terms for collective discourse. Sixty-three per cent of the actions were of this kind, as were 34 per cent of the statements.

If the perspective were not held collectively, we would not expect to discover so many incidents in which its terms could be used in conversation without provoking argument, dissent, or expressions of disbelief. Nor would we expect to find so many actions occurring in which the premises contained in the perspective could be used, without discussion, as the basis for collective action. That they are so used, without argument or difficulty, indicates that they are so commonly held as to be assumed, unquestioningly, as something that any reasonable student would be likely to know and understand.

NEGATIVE CASES

We have now reviewed the evidence that indicates that the grade point average perspective was frequent and widely held, as well as evidence supporting the proposition that it is customary and a matter of consensus among students. Our review of this evidence, however, would not be complete without considering the possibility and the existence of negative cases.

In the analysis of perspectives, a negative case is an incident in which students indicate that they do not accept or act on the premises of the perspective being analyzed, in this case the grade point average perspective. If we use a strict criterion for negative cases, we include only those incidents in which students explicitly denounce the grade point average perspective in favor of some other perspective or instances in which they take actions clearly at odds with it. If we use a looser and more inclusive

been so distributed among all the categories mentioned, for this would have created an impossibly difficult sampling problem. In any case, we did not attempt it, for we were more interested in some students than others; thus we spent a disproportionate amount of time with leaders of campus organizations. Since we could not make a strong test of our proposition that the perspective was widespread, we have relied on the weak test of checking that instances of the perspective's use were discovered in every subdivision of every category.

criterion, we include incidents in which students act to maximize some valuable other than grades. The difficulty in using the more inclusive criterion is that the student statements or actions being reviewed frequently do not specifically indicate a rejection of the grade point average perspective. Rather, they show that students are able, under certain circumstances, to operate on another set of premises. One can use either criterion, but in neither case is the number of instances sufficient to cast doubt on the existence or ubiquity of the GPA perspective.

Professional Orientations. In fourteen items, students evinced an interest in their courses from the point of view of how what they were learning related to the professional futures they envisioned for themselves. They spoke of how what they were learning in class would be useful either in graduate school or in the occupations they intended to take up when they left college. For instance, a student majoring in history said that he wanted to become a politician and thought that knowing how things happened in the past would be useful for making speeches. Another student had decided not only in which field he would do graduate work, but which school he would attend and on what subject he would write his dissertation; he chose term papers so that they would help him prepare the groundwork for the dissertation.

Incidents of this kind suggest the possibility of an alternative perspective, in which one would make judgments and take actions according to how well one was being prepared for an envisioned professional future and would recognize this as the chief valuable to be gained from academic work. Twelve of the fourteen items mentioned give no evidence of such an alternative perspective, indicating only that the students involved here have interests in addition to grades in their course work. There is no indication that the interest in a professional future provides the entire framework of belief and action characteristic of the GPA perspective. It remains a personal interest, grafted onto the GPA perspective and operating only when the two do not conflict.

Two incidents, however, provide more serious negations of our proposition. In one, a student argues that he learns a great deal from businessmen who come to address a departmental club to which he belongs, a great deal more than he could learn in his classes. In the other, a student in journalism speaks glowingly of learning repertorial techniques, because they will stand him in good stead when he becomes a professional newspaperman. In both cases, the students clearly imply that what they learn in this fashion is of such importance that they would, if necessary, give up grades for the sake of the knowledge. (In only one of the cases, however, did it seem likely that the student would ever have to face this contingency.)

We can only speculate as to why this alternative perspective does not occur more frequently. It may be because very few of the students have any clear conception of what their future occupational roles will be. Such an orientation may become more common when the student is in graduate school. (We found just such an orientation common among medical students.[3]) Or it may be that, insofar as students do have some notion of what their professional future may be, they see no conflict between the kind of learning imposed on them by the requirements of their courses and what they will need to know to practice their chosen occupations. They may assume that if they do well in their classes they will necessarily be learning whatever it is they will need to know in the future.[4]

A Liberal Arts Orientation. Students might also accept an orientation we ascribed earlier to many college teachers, one that might be called the "liberal arts perspective." A student holding such a perspective might, for instance, view his academic experiences as opportunities to open himself to new ideas, new emotions, and new ways of looking at the world. He might proceed to pick his courses, choose his reading, and do the other things to which he would devote his time and effort on this basis. In fact, we find in our field notes fifty-one incidents in which students express something like this perspective.

But in almost every case the incident makes clear that the liberal arts perspective on academic work, like the professional orientation perspective, is something "extra," something to be engaged in (indulged in might be a more exact term) when nothing else interferes, particularly when there is no pressure for grades. Sometimes the student puts it this way: he hopes to get this kind of value out of his course work, even though he understands clearly that it must take second place.

[3] Becker et al., *op. cit.*, pp. 221–273.

[4] Trow and Clark argue that, contrary to what our analysis shows, such a vocational orientation is quite common in American colleges. Our differing conclusions may be due, though we doubt it, to differences between the University of Kansas and the schools they have in mind. They may be due to differences between the modes of data gathering that we have used and those that they suggest; that is, the differences might result from a difference between what one gets from participant observation and what one gets from survey data. In some large part, however, they are due to a difference in what is meant by "perspective" on the one hand and "orientation" on the other. In studying perspectives, we look at ongoing interaction in a social situation. In studying orientations, we study attitudes that may not, for structural reasons, have a chance to be expressed in collective action.

One may espouse a particular orientation without being able to put it into practice, because of institutional constraints. We believe that many students may espouse vocational ideals but that, nevertheless, if they are on a campus like Kansas where grades are institutionalized as the chief valuable, they will of necessity use the GPA perspective (or something like it) in practice. See Burton R. Clark and Martin Trow, "The Organizational Context," in Theodore M. Newcomb and Everett R. Wilson, eds., *College Peer Groups* (Chicago: Aldine Publishing Co., 1966), pp. 17–70.

In addition to being stated explicitly by students, the liberal arts perspective also appears in activities that seem to be undertaken to further the goal of having new experiences. Thus, just as we noted that many students have no books on their shelves other than textbooks, we saw some other students who had large collections of books in many fields, most of them unrelated to their current course work. Or we observed students attending classes largely because they felt the teacher was "interesting" or reading books or engaging in activities that were not related to their course work but had the same "interesting" quality.

What is characteristic of these activities is that they are largely undertaken by students who have the time to spare for them because they have their ordinary course work well under control. It is the brightest students who have many books on their shelves, the brightest students who engage in scholastic bull sessions. This supports the interpretation that the liberal arts perspective is something *added* to the grade point average perspective, rather than something that *replaces* it. Viewed this way, instances of activity oriented to a liberal arts perspective do not constitute negative cases to the grade point average perspective, for there is no real conflict between them. The student does not have to choose between doing something for one set of reasons and doing something for the other set of reasons; he finishes his academically required course work and, in the time his abilities make available to him, goes on to have "liberal arts experiences."

One kind of activity is an exception to this rule. A few professors in the University have achieved a campus reputation of being "interesting." The sources of this interest deserve more study than we have given them. They seem to have in common, however, that they deal with "big ideas" in their lectures and that they range widely across several fields of knowledge. Be that as it may, many students take their courses or, if they feel they cannot afford the extra work, sit in on the courses without taking them for credit. Some of the students who do this are not as well off academically as the others we have mentioned who undertake actions based on the liberal arts perspective. On the other hand, to take one course of this kind for one semester is not, when considered in the perspective of a total college career, very much of a deviation from the grade point average perspective.

Thus, although we have fifty-one incidents that reflect in one way or another the liberal arts perspective, we find none that constitute truly negative cases with respect to the grade point average perspective. It may be objected that we have made our criterion excessively strict, and there is something to this objection. For instance, we judged it as a positive instance, favoring the proposition that students have the grade point average perspective, when we saw nothing but textbooks on a student's shelf. On the other hand, we did not regard it as a negative instance when we saw books other than textbooks on his shelf. It is by this kind of one-way strictness that we conclude that there are no negative cases in this category. If, however, we use a very loose criterion we still have only fifty-one negative cases as compared with more than one thousand positive instances. Therefore, we can at most conclude that the liberal arts perspective is held by a small minority of students. If our data gave us systematic information on situations of conflict between either the professional or liberal arts perspective and the grade point average perspective, we could say definitely in how many cases we have truly negative findings. Lacking such definitive evidence, we can only say that at best these are minority points of view.

Truly Negative Cases. Finally, we have eleven incidents in which students simply say they are not particularly interested in grades and will not go out of their way to get a good grade; or, alternatively, that they do not think that grades are really very important, do not care whether members of their living group get good grades or not, and so on.

In three instances, the most outspoken expressions, the students involved are in either journalism or fine arts. It seems likely that their relative lack of interest in courses, grades, and degrees is related to the fact that a professional future in these fields does not require a college degree. In two other cases, the students involved in the incident come from living groups only tangentially related to the social and cultural life of the campus community. The other six cases involved quite bright students who had no trouble with their grades, but seemed to regard it as a matter hardly deserving attention. They were quite firm in their insistence that, although they got high grades, this was not a matter of any real importance to them.

Thus using a strict criterion we have only thirteen negative instances (two of a professional orientation and the eleven truly negative cases). Using a loose criterion we have a total of seventy-six (fourteen professional, fifty-one liberal arts, and eleven truly negative). In either case, comparison with the total number of positive instances indicates that students use the grade point average perspective overwhelmingly in approaching their academic work.

CHAPTER **10**

CONCLUSION

When we apply the sociological perspective to specific areas of human activity, we invariably find that what had been thought to be matters of individual judgment, motivation, and action have a collective character. Industrial workers do not so much respond to changes in wages or working conditions according to their own individual feelings and beliefs as they arrive at a collective judgment about the best course of action in the altered work situation.[1] Response to medical treatment depends less on the individual psychology of patients than on the relation between the healers and the sick.[2] The actions of deviants stem less from their personalities than from the complex interactions between them, other deviants, and agents of social control.[3]

In speaking of the collective character of action we do not refer to a simple model in which, let us say, workers discuss and agree on restrictive norms of production. Rather, when we speak of action as collective we refer to the joint action of *all* the people involved: managers *and* workers, doctors *and* patients, police *and* deviants. The collective act, that all parties involved jointly produce, interests us: what workers do in the context of the relations between them and all the others with whom they interact at work, what patients do in the context of their relations with other patients, doctors, and nurses.

Though sociological research always discovers that human action is collective, the discovery always needs to be made anew, for members of

[1] F. V. Roethlisberger and W. J. Dixon, *Management and the Worker* (Cambridge, Mass.: Harvard University Press, 1939), and William F. Whyte and Melville Dalton, *Money and Motivation* (New York: Harper, 1955).
[2] See the review of relevant research in Eliot Freidson, "Health Factories: The New Industrial Sociology," *Social Problems,* 14 (Spring, 1967), pp. 493–500.
[3] David Matza, *Delinquency and Drift* (New York: John Wiley and Sons, 1964), and Howard S. Becker, *Outsiders* (Glencoe, Ill.: The Free Press, 1963).

one kind of organization usually do not see the underlying similarities between organizations that the sociologist's theory suggests to him. Doctors do not automatically apply the results of industrial research to their problems with patients; police do not apply the same results to their problems with deviants. In fact, the people who run the major institutions of society typically resist this insight. They prefer to believe that the actions of those they deal with can be understood on an individual basis and that their own professional actions can best be organized on that premise.

The reasons for the preference lie beyond the scope of our study, but one seems especially important. If we ignore the collective character of actions for whose control we are responsible, we can likewise ignore our own complicity in producing those actions. If we locate the responsibility for everything that happens in the individuals we work with, by making everything that happens a function of *their* attributes—*their* abilities or interests or motives—we hide our own contribution to the shaping of what they do. That contribution usually results from well-established patterns of institutional organization in which people acquire vested interests. Change is painful. We can more comfortably ignore what we do, regard it as something given and fixed, and look for sources of trouble and potential for change in the subordinate participants in our institutions.[4]

In any event, we have once again discovered that what looks like a matter of individual effort—the academic performance of college students—is really collective. The finding has a double import. It gives us a new viewpoint from which to assess the problems colleges confront in carrying out their academic mission. It also allows us to suggest some sociological propositions about the activities of subordinate groups in hierarchically organized institutions.

As we have indicated earlier, college faculty typically see their interaction with students as an individual matter. The teacher presents material and attempts to interest students in it so that they will devote their effort to learning what he wants them to know. If they do not learn, it is because they do not have the ability to do so or because the teacher has insufficiently interested them.

But the faculty view is faulty. It assumes that student performance depends solely on ability and interest and ignores the complicated network of social relations, group definitions, and obligations in which students find themselves. It sees student performance as a simple response to the professor's offerings rather than as the construction of a complex line of

---

[4] For a related argument, see Howard S. Becker, "Whose Side Are We On?" *Social Problems,* 14 (Winter, 1967), pp. 239–247.

action in a complicated and demanding social setting. It underestimates students' rationality in attempting to meet and satisfy the many demands made on them. It fails, in short, to give full weight to the socially structured conditions of student performance.

THE CONDITIONS OF STUDENT ACTION

The most important condition influencing students' academic activity is their relationship of subjection to faculty and administration. Rules governing academic work are made unilaterally, the administration setting the terms on which students can remain in school and engage in a variety of other available activities, and the faculty setting the work to be done and evaluating its adequacy. Most important, the faculty and administration have institutionalized grades as the only formal means by which performance is assessed. In addition, the college organizes and schedules academic work in a way that reflects the decision to so use grades: the length of courses, the assignments given, testing procedures, and so on all reflect the necessity of giving grades according to the system in use. Furthermore, grades, ostensibly commensurable across graders and available for all students, tend to be used as a means of distinguishing among students for all sorts of other purposes. This links many other rewards and valuables to students' academic performance, so that low grades restrict opportunities in other areas of college life while making the grade academically opens the way to further rewards.

A second condition influences students' academic perspectives. Even under the condition of subjection, they can still act collectively. While faculty and administration make the rules, they do not attempt to create a situation in which students have no contact with one another and thus cannot act collectively. (Such a situation is found, for example, in prisons that make use of solitary confinement. It might be noted, though, that officials find it difficult, in even the most strictly run institution, to enforce rules preventing communication and collective action.[5])

Collective action is possible in another sense. The University is so organized that most of the students live in close proximity and are, by virtue of their other activities, brought together frequently; they have, in addition, time available in which to interact. So they can act collectively as they could not, for instance, in a commuter college in which most students scatter as soon as classes end, having neither the time nor the locale for interaction.[6]

[5] See Richard McCleery, "Authoritarianism and the Belief System of Incorrigibles," in Donald J. Cressey, ed., *The Prison* (New York: Holt, Rinehart & Winston, 1961), pp. 260–306.
[6] For a discussion of the importance of interaction possibilities in the development of collective forms of action, see Howard S. Becker, Blanche Geer, Everett C. Hughes,

Since students can and do interact, they can share perspectives on their academic problems. They can arrive at common definitions of their situation and give shared meanings to the people and contingencies they confront. Because they share definitions and meanings, they can develop coordinated lines of action, acting together in ways that help them deal with their problems of academic work. If, for example, they define grades as a measure of organizational prestige, they can then act together to raise the grades of an organization's members, since all those members agree on what the problem is and in what direction a solution must be sought. As we have seen, KU students take advantage of these opportunities and not only can but do engage in collective action.

Given their position of loose subjection and their capacity for collective action, students have a certain amount of autonomy in organizing and carrying out their own affairs. They can, to a degree, choose among alternative courses of action. That autonomy is, of course, limited. They cannot choose, for instance, not to have grades. Nor can they choose to attend any class they want for as long or short a period as they want. But, within the limits set by the organization of the University and the campus, given the problems and conditions of action that organization presents, they can choose alternative strategies and alternative allocations of effort.

In making their choices, students find that the organization of academic life allows them to deviate from some of the ideals and standards held by faculty and administration. The opportunity to deviate arises from the disjunction between those ideals and standards and the mechanisms that have been created and institutionalized to realize them, the disjunction, for instance, between a system of courses, credits, and grades and the conventional aims of a liberal education. By obeying the dictates of that system, students not only can but in a real sense must deviate from those aims. They deviate as well even from the aims implicit in the grade system, by adopting strategies designed to get grades rather than to acquire the knowledge grades supposedly represent. They deviate most, perhaps, by refusing to accept the premise implicit in both the conventional structure and the idealized aims, the premise that the student's major effort and first priority in college must go to academic work.

Deviation of all these kinds is possible not only because controls over students are loose enough to allow it, but also because students feel justified in their deviant activities. The justification arises from the collective character of what is done. Few people will deliberately disobey an order whose legitimacy everyone accepts. It is quite another thing to do

and Anselm L. Strauss, *Boys in White: Student Culture in Medical School* (Chicago: University of Chicago Press, 1961), pp. 135–157.

something that, however it may look to superiors in an organization, has been defined by most people one knows as reasonable, a sensible thing to do in the circumstances. When one knows that what he thinks and does accords with "what everybody knows," deviance is easier. Indeed, to violate that commonsense view takes courage.

Under the conditions of loose subjection, collective action, and relative autonomy, then, students arrive at their perspective on academic work.

THE GPA PERSPECTIVE

The preceding chapters have described in detail the perspective KU students actually used in the academic area. Without repeating or summarizing that material, we can emphasize certain of its broad features.

The GPA perspective takes the rules made by faculty and administration about academic work as the basic reality with which a student must deal. It accepts as the definition of what is important the judgments handed down unilaterally from above and, in so doing, accepts the relationship of subjection between students and University without question. It accepts, of course, the definition embodied in college practice—the definition that makes grades the measure of academic achievement—and not various other definitions offered by University spokesmen from time to time which are not embodied in authoritative practice.

Given this definition of what is important, the GPA perspective indicates various actions appropriate for students: seeking information, working hard, attempting to manipulate faculty in order to get a better grade, organizing for collective action to improve the chances of getting a good grade, allocating effort in such a way as to maximize the overall GPA, and so on. In short, students do what they calculate will best enable them to make the grade in what the institution proffers as the only impersonal, objective, and formally recognized way of making that assessment.

The student emphasis on grades arises, then, in response to an academic environment that also emphasizes grades. In a relationship of subjection in which the higher echelon dictates what will be institutionalized as valuable, making and enforcing rules to implement that choice, members of the lower echelon must, if they are to act effectively and remain members of the organization, accept that judgment and shape their own actions accordingly. Any other line of action is futile, perhaps romantic, for neglecting to reckon with institutionalized practice produces failure as that is institutionally defined. Students who do not take grades seriously flunk out or suffer serious disabilities, academic and other. They cannot get from their college experience what they or any other responsible person considers important for them to get.

But—and it is a big but—the influence of institutional rules extends only so far. The faculty may believe that students should put major, if not exclusive, emphasis on academic work, though perhaps not the kind of emphasis on grades we have described as characteristic. Students see things differently. They believe that, *within* the area of academic work, major emphasis must be put on grades. But they believe that other areas of activity are important too—the areas of organizational activity and personal relationships—and that the value of the rewards to be gained through academic effort must be weighed against the rewards that might be realized through other kinds of activity.

Indeed, students' generalized goal of maturity comes to have as its specific reference a proper balancing of effort in all three areas. When students speak approvingly of someone as being "all-round," they mean to applaud his ability to keep things in proper balance, neither overdoing nor underplaying the value of any of the three.

In balancing their responsibilities, obligations, and opportunities, students do not underestimate the importance of academic work. They understand and take into account that some minimal level of academic performance is necessary before rewards can be sought in other areas. But they sometimes decide—and this is where their views diverge most from those of faculty—that they will settle for a lower level of academic achievement than they could expect if they devoted all their effort to academic work, choosing instead to pursue other rewards they also consider important. A student who decides to settle for a B average so that he can devote more time to campus political activities, in some part so that his fraternity house will benefit, may, from the faculty point of view, be acting immaturely and irresponsibly. But students think him mature, because he understands that the benefits he will gain from political activity are important too, and responsible because he helps his fraternity brothers through his own activity. It is likely (though we have no way of making such an estimate) that many students deliberately, in this sense, "underachieve" academically so that they may gain benefits in other areas of campus life.

Students' academic activities can be understood, then, by dropping the faculty viewpoint that sees what they do as a function of ability and interest and placing those activities instead in the more complicated social context we have described. Students do not respond to the teacher alone or to the lure of his subject matter. They respond to him only after they assess what a reasonable course of action vis-à-vis him would be, given other demands, academic and extra-academic, made on them and given the definitions and understandings about academic achievement current among their peers. Student academic performance is, in this extended sense, collective action and can be understood by being seen as such.

SOME SOCIOLOGICAL CONCLUSIONS

We have described students' perspective on academic work and suggested the conditions under which it emerges. It is clear that the GPA perspective is a way of looking at one's academic work that will not make many college faculty members happy. But it is a reasonable response to the way colleges do business. By exploring that logical connection we can arrive at some sociological conclusions about the control of behavior in relationships of subjection.

Let us take as given, for the moment, that we want to expand faculty control so that students will do what faculty want. That requires us to assume, unrealistically, that faculty could agree on what they want of students. But, for a start, let us assume that they have accepted our analysis and want to increase student devotion to academic work, redirecting it from simply acquiring grades toward a scholarly interest in academic studies for their own sake. What would we have to do to achieve that end? Which is another way of asking what in the present situation prevents the realization of those aims.

This proposition suggests itself: those who control an institution—the superordinates—can control the behavior of subordinate groups to the degree that they control *all* sources of reward valued by subordinates and make *all* those rewards depend on doing what is wanted.[7] If some sources of reward escape this coordination (as is bound to happen in even the most totalitarian arrangement, let alone in an organization as loosely controlled as a university), subordinates will balance the rewards to be gained by doing what their superiors want against the rewards that can be gained by evading or ignoring those demands. The existence of alternative rewards sets the stage for systematic allocation of effort in alternative directions, as subordinates use their autonomy to settle for a little less of what superiors can provide in return for a little more of what is not under their direct control.

Add now the proposition that superordinates can maximize their control by arranging institutionally controlled rewards so that every additional increment of effort by subordinates is rewarded by a commensurable increment in reward. If they do not arrange rewards in this way but rather, as is commonly done, tie the most potent sanctions to the achievement of some minimum standard, many subordinates will settle for that minimal level of performance and reward, ignoring the relatively smaller additional rewards to be gained from a further investment of

[7] The problem of the autonomy of subordinates is discussed in David Mechanic, "Sources of Power of Lower Participants in Complex Organizations," *Administrative Science Quarterly*, 7 (December, 1962), pp. 349–364.

effort. In the economist's language, superiors can maximize control by making the marginal utility of each additional increment of effort equal rather than decreasing.

Consider finally this proposition. A system of control produces the desired results only if superordinates devise a system of assessing and evaluating what subordinates do accurately enough so that they can reward only those actions they want to reward and no others. Superordinates cannot control behavior unless they know when the actions they want have been performed and when they have not. A system of evaluation is ineffective if it allows subordinates to produce the appearance of satisfactory performance without the substance. Superordinates find it difficult to devise efficient evaluation systems, particularly when what is to be controlled is the level and direction of effort that subordinates bring to their tasks. (A vast literature devoted to this problem has grown up in the field of industrial relations, where managers search for ways to measure and control workers' productive effort.)

We have drawn these abstract propositions, by induction, from our study of student academic effort. Let us bring them down to earth by relating them to the specifics of college life. If a college faculty and administration want greater student conformity to their academic goals, they must move much farther in the direction of controlling all sources of those rewards students find valuable, linking achievement of the rewards to the academic activity they desire. They must control access to the valuables to be gained in organizational activity and personal relationships and so arrange matters that those valuables can be gained only by increased student effort in the desired direction. Furthermore, assuming that grades continue to be used as the chief reward for academic performance, they must extend the range of grades so that bright students cannot achieve the top reward with less than full effort. They must also make the reward values of various levels of grades more commensurable, not clustering maximum increments of value around, for instance, a C level GPA, thus allowing students who achieve that to relax, relieved that they have made it sufficient for their purposes. Finally, they must make grades reflect student effort and achievement more accurately than they now do, so that the "clever grade-getter" will vanish as a type.

Our sociological conclusions may provide forthright advice on how to achieve faculty ends more adequately, but they do not provide practical advice. No American university, whose students attend voluntarily, whose income comes from outside sources, and whose faculty believe in democracy in some form or another, would be willing or able to take the steps needed to implement that advice. Nor would they have the expertise necessary to devise an evaluation system that would make it workable. Not even a totalitarian state would have all the necessary means; an American university would have neither the means nor the will. A totalitarian system might go a long way toward achieving total control by following our recipe. But few American universities would be willing to take even the few steps toward the control of matters we consider private business that would allow some greater measure of control over academic performance. American faculty members typically denigrate the value and importance of organizational activity and personal relationships in college life, but few would be willing to enlarge their control over them beyond what now exists.

WHAT CAN THE FACULTY DO?

The preceding discussion assumed as a goal increasing student conformity to faculty and administration views of how students ought to act in the academic area. But we made that assumption for analytic purposes only, to make the import of our argument clearer, not because we accept it ourselves. There are reasons not to accept it.

One reason not to accept the goal of increasing conformity to faculty desires is that faculty desires vary so much that no very coherent plan could be developed from them. Faculties debate educational policy interminably, to their credit; they want to do their job as well as reason and ability allow. But they seldom agree, except on the most general statements of principle, and even fight over those when they perceive that implications with which they might disagree could be drawn from them. Faculty members differ over ends: the inculcation of skills and information or the student's personal development? They differ over means: quarters or semesters? Lectures or discussions? The reasons for these differences, worthy of study in their own right, need not concern us. But their tenacious survival, through decades of committee meetings and faculty reports, suggests that they will not soon disappear, hence that the goal of increasing conformity to faculty desires is in principle unachievable because no unitary goal can be defined.

Supposing that faculty unanimity could be achieved, however, there is another reason for rejecting the goal of increasing student conformity. The students' academic perspective suggests that faculty fail to accord sufficient importance to nonacademic activities, seeing them either as totally useless or all right in their place, a distant second to academic work. We think students assess faculty views correctly in this matter and that they correctly judge them to be one-sided. We have not, in this volume, analyzed what it is that students find so valuable in organizational activity and personal relationships. We can only assert that they do find value there, leaving the documentation and analysis to later publications, and that they present substantial arguments in support of that view.[8]

We have argued, then, that the goal of increasing student conformity to faculty views of how they should behave academically is not a worthy one and that, in any case, few American universities would be able to make even the tentative steps toward implementing the goal our analysis suggests. What can be proposed instead, if one wants to change colleges for the better?

Let us abandon the goal of manipulating students into doing what the faculty desires and settle for something more modest. We can take as a reasonable proximate goal that we at least do nothing (or as little as possible) to interfere with whatever tendency students might have to engage in academic activities, whether they are defined as the acquisition of knowledge and skill, the pursuit of intellectual and scholarly interests, personal development, or whatever. Instead of trying to get students to do what we want, we look only for ways of not encouraging them to do what we do not want. We ask how a college might be organized so as not to provoke or coerce students into forms of activity that interfere with what we might want to achieve.[9]

That is a perhaps disappointingly modest goal. It is, nevertheless, a possibly attainable one. Our sociological analysis suggests ways of reaching it and, though these would be politically difficult, they do not seem as unrealizable as what we have already considered.

Our analysis of the GPA perspective suggests that, as things stand, the chief obstacle to a more scholarly approach by students to their academic studies is their belief that they must give first priority to the pursuit of grades. The chief condition for the existence of that perspective is the institutionalization of grades as the reward for academic effort, and the linking of rewards in other areas as well to grades. If we deemphasize or abolish grading systems, the calculation of grade point averages, and their use as a way of discriminating among students, we destroy a major obstacle to academic activity. Students would not devote their time to finding out what the instructor wants, or to attempting to produce the appearance without the substance of knowledge, or to many of

[8] For some preliminary statements on these points, see the references cited in footnote 2, p. 3.
[9] This is not to say that an instructor would not still desire certain kinds of response from students and therefore would try to retain his position of dominance over the class, for there is good reason to suppose that he would. (See Blanche Geer, "Teaching," *International Encyclopedia of the Social Sciences,* Vol. 15, pp. 560–565.) Many, perhaps most, instructors now use grades to achieve this end. If grades were abolished, they might devise other ways to accomplish the same end, and these might, in turn, produce other kinds of unwanted and unintended consequences. For this reason, the changes suggested here might have less effect than we argue they will.

the other activities that now frustrate and annoy their teachers. Freed of the necessity to cater to faculty demands as they can divine them, students might turn to activities more in line with faculty desires.[10]

That does not mean that they *would* turn their efforts in that direction. Freed of the necessity to get grades, they would not automatically desire to become scholars; but those who have such desires would be free to pursue them. Those who want to avoid work would, of course, be free to do so. But faculty members might consider whether they are not willing to pay that price, for by definition such students are now motivated solely by grades; it is an open question how much they learn, beyond what is necessary to pass an examination or squeeze a term paper through, and no question at all that they provide most instructors with their greatest sense of failure. In addition, freed of the anxiety and fear of failure provoked by the grading system, some students might discover new and more scholarly or intellectual motives for action.

Other objections can be raised to our modest proposal. We need grades, it is sometimes said, so that employers, graduate schools, and other consumers of the college's product can distinguish among students in order to choose which ones they will recruit. Granted that consumers need to make distinctions, should the university do the job for them? In fact, the use of grades for such purposes only compounds the educational difficulties grades create, by making them important not only for one's campus life but for one's vocational future as well. Faculty members had this dramatically called to their attention when a student's academic rank, based on grades, became a partial basis for draft board decisions to call men into military service. At that point, a good many faculty members decided that they did not want to do that particular job of discriminating among students for an outside consumer. But there is no good reason to do it for any consumer, if a by-product is a substantial obstacle to a more intellectual or scholarly perspective among students. Employers and graduate schools could work out their own devices for picking among college graduates, and giving up this task would not interfere with the college's educational mission.

Some faculty members will object that they need examinations and similar devices to know how well their students are doing. We do not suggest that any teacher who finds such means useful give them up. We only suggest that the results of such procedures be restricted to the instructor's pedagogical use, and not be communicated to a central office to be kept on record and, combined with other grades, made the basis for other decisions about the student. If teachers did not, in any case,

[10] Paul Goodman has made similar proposals. See his *The Community of Scholars* (New York: Random House, 1962), especially pp. 91–97.

have to turn in grades every semester or quarter in a standard form, they might find it possible to devise more effective ways of making the same judgments.

Some faculty members will agree that, given present testing and grading practices, what we say is true, but that better examining procedures could be devised that would meet some of our objections. We might make a strong effort to develop tests that measure more adequately than we presently do precisely those skills and knowledge we wish students to acquire. Most instructors now construct tests in a haphazard and uninformed way, devoting insufficient time and attention to such a serious matter. We probably could construct tests that would tap more directly the relevant skills and knowledge. But such an effort, we think, would be self-limiting. The easiest form of examination to grade—both in time and lack of arguable ambiguities—is the multiple-choice test. But it is notoriously difficult to construct multiple-choice examinations that tap what we are really after. We are more likely to be satisfied with essays or papers as true indicators of what a student knows; but essays and papers take much longer to grade and the standards by which we judge them are complex and ambiguous. The more effective an examining procedure, the more it will have these qualities; few faculty members can afford the time or bear the ambiguities connected with a really good examining procedure.

We might reform examining procedures in another direction by separating the jobs of teaching and examining, setting up a separate board of examiners to make whatever assessments need to be made, leaving the instructor free to teach without the burden of grades. Under such a system, properly run, students know that their instructor cannot have any influence on their grades and cannot tell them about the content of the evaluation procedures used. Some teachers, of course, might not wish to let things get so much out of their hands. Students would still have grades to worry about, with all the attendant difficulties, but that worry, at least, would not intrude into the classroom or into their relations with faculty.

At present, grading systems are receiving much attention, and changes of various kinds are being made. The most common innovation is the substitution of a pass-fail system for letter grades, either across the board or, more commonly, in a limited number of courses, usually outside the student's major. Some preliminary evidence suggests that students like the change.[11] It decreases the pressure on them, allows them to explore fields in which they are intellectually interested but had not previously

[11] See "Pass-Fail Grading," *Memo to the Faculty* (from the Center for Research on Teaching and Learning, University of Michigan), No. 22 (April, 1967).

pursued for fear of effecting adversely their GPA or for other reasons.

Pass-fail seems a useful half-measure, useful in proportion to the number of courses it covers and thus to its effect on a student's grade point average. If we restrict use of the system to a few courses, it will simply provide a sort of breathing space for students and an opportunity for a little preliminary exploration of fields outside the major. If, however, we grade all or most courses in this fashion, we begin to destroy the usefulness of the GPA as a way of distinguishing among students. While some students might fail frequently enough to mark them out as a special group, the overall GPA's of most students would probably become relatively indistinguishable, thus making it difficult or impossible to use the GPA as it is presently used. This would go a long way toward removing the connection between grades and other sources of reward now so prevalent. The pressure to get passing grades, no small pressure for a large number of students, would remain unchanged.

A similar halfway measure might be to give grades, but to keep them unavailable for all except strictly academic purposes. Students could still flunk out or fail to graduate on the basis of their grades, but grades would otherwise not be public. They could not be used to decide questions of organizational membership or officeholding, for example, nor would they be available to prospective employers or graduate schools. Such a move would, again, do away with some difficulties that now exist.

But half-measures are half-measures. Far better to experiment boldly with total abolition, spending our energies not in patching up an old and unworkable system but in devising ways of meeting the unforeseen problems that any new system will produce. To abolish grades will be a difficult matter, for many administrators and faculty members believe firmly in their utility. Yet some colleges are now making such experiments, which suggests that under some circumstances resistance can be overcome.[12] That abolition is possible should not be surprising; it is certainly an easier innovation to introduce than those extensions of college control over student behavior we discussed earlier. While it attacks many traditional practices and vested interests and will create many new problems, it does not involve any violations of democratic principles or procedures and will probably create much less antagonism among students and other constituencies of the university.

[12] *Ibid.*, p. 3, summarizes the experiments currently under way.

THE STUDENTS' POINT OF VIEW

So far we have approached the problem of students' academic effort from a faculty point of view, asking what measures a faculty might take to influence students to behave in ways that are, from that standpoint, desirable. We concluded that the best the faculty could do might be to at least refrain from interfering with students' scholarly and intellectual activities, and that they might best do this by getting rid of grading systems.

However, we can also look at the problem from the students' side, and, indeed, our stance in this volume obligates us to do that. But we face a severe difficulty in the attempt—the difficulty of specifying in what direction students might look for a desirable change. Students, as the evidence we have presented shows, by and large accept the university's system of grading so completely that they cannot conceive effective alternatives to it. In particular, they believe, with few exceptions, that grades do measure something worth measuring, that in general they measure it accurately, and that it is entirely appropriate to tie rewards in other areas of campus life to academic achievement as that is reflected in grades. In their acceptance of these premises, students exhibit most nakedly the influence of their position of subjection vis-à-vis the faculty and administration.

On the other hand, students aross the country increasingly demand a voice in university affairs. Although they have tended to focus their complaints around political activity and university regulation of student extracurricular behavior, the time will surely come when they will want a voice in the organization and regulation of academic affairs as well. As of now, such dissatisfaction finds its expression in the establishment of Free Universities on the fringes of the conventional university. We sense that if students were to gain a voice in academic affairs, they would have no coherent program or point of view to present and thus would be easy targets for conservative faculty members who already doubt the wisdom of student participation. As a result of our study, we can perhaps suggest what some worthwhile student goals might be, as well as some possible ways of achieving them.

Students might want any or all of several things out of the university's system for managing academic matters. They may, for example, want to acquire the knowledge their professors have in their own subject matter, be that technical or cultural knowledge. They may want to master the calculus, learn to read and enjoy literature, acquire a working knowledge of a foreign language, or learn the results and methods of work of some science. They may desire that knowledge out of scholarly curiosity, because they believe they will need it in their future work or professional training, because they want to become more rounded human beings, or because it is what they are ready for at their stage of personal development. Whatever the reason, knowledge is one thing students might reasonably ask of their academic work.

Students may desire the academic program to provide them with a challenge, with a test of their ability to perform adequately under conditions they consider adult. They may want to use the program as a way of checking whether, in doing their academic work, they exhibit the qualities they believe necessary for occupational success: initiative, intellectual ability, persistence, and so on. Many students find the present grading system an adequate way of testing whether they have met the challenge posed by their courses, which they consider a sufficient challenge.

Students may also want the university's academic program to provide motivation for them. Many students recognize that while knowledge is desirable, acquiring it is hard work; they fear that their own desire for knowledge is not strong enough to lead them to exert the necessary effort. From this point of view, the university ought to provide some built-in motivation in the way it allocates rewards and punishments. If the sanctions are severe enough, students reason, we will do what we ought to do for our own good but might otherwise leave undone. If we are graded in class, and those grades have fateful consequences for other things we want to accomplish, we will work and acquire the knowledge we want to have. Students might thus demand that the university supply the push to do academic work they cannot supply themselves.

Many students, particularly those in positions that require them to make discriminations among their fellows, find the system tremendously useful in doing that job. The members of a sorority find first-semester grades a useful way of choosing among prospective pledges; the officers of campus organizations find the GPA a useful way of deciding which students to entrust with important tasks. Some students, then, want the system to provide, as it now does, ways of making these choices.

Students may also desire relief from those sanctions when they become too onerous. They may wish to be able to try courses and subjects without running the risk of such severe sanctions as being forced to leave school, being unable to join a fraternity or sorority, or being unable to hold office in campus organizations.

Finally, students may want to retain some freedom of choice with respect to the amount of effort they devote to academic work. They may want to be able to say that they will devote only the necessary minimum of effort to academic work, in order that they be free to spend time with a girl friend, take part in campus politics, devote themselves to the affairs of their house, or whatever.

Clearly, the present system already goes far toward maximizing some of these goals. It provides motivation for a large number of students, and a great deal of freedom of choice with respect to the allocation of effort for many. Many students get the knowledge they want. The system shows its greatest weakness in meeting the criterion of relief from onerous sanctions.

However, the present system just as clearly creates grave difficulties for many students who find that, under it, the attempt to maximize two or more of these goals fails. For example, as we have seen, some students feel a strong conflict between gaining knowledge and avoiding the sanctions of the grading system. If they follow their desire for knowledge, they neglect some of the tasks they must perform if they are to get good grades; if they make their grades, they feel that they have sacrificed some possibilities of intellectual growth to the system. Other students find that they do not have the freedom to engage in other kinds of campus activities because of the necessity of meeting minimum academic requirements in order to avoid sanctions. Many students consider themselves perfectly capable of furnishing their own motivation. Though no student suffers from all these difficulties, enough suffer from one or more of them for us to ask whether, from a student point of view, the system could be changed in some way that might diminish them.

To begin our answer to that question, we can note that the student body can be divided into segments according to the kind of trouble they have with the present system. A top group of students has no difficulty at all with academic requirements. They can do any assignment likely to be given in a college class with ease and a sure knowledge that they can earn an A if they want to. Such students often try to fashion a more serious challenge for themselves by taking more than the usual number of hours, a double or triple major, or a greater number of upper-level or even graduate courses, seeing whether, even with this handicap, they can maintain a high GPA. Sometimes, however, they try to follow an independent course of study, pursuing in depth those topics that seem to them most important, and it is this pursuit that the conventional system sometimes interferes with. Some of these bright students feel, as well, that they do not require incentives like grades to make them work; they regard the system as childish and degrading.

A second group of students, no doubt the largest, consists of students who find the present system a real challenge, but a manageable one. They believe that they need the motivation it provides; they find it useful and important as a way of running campus organizations; they feel that they acquire the knowledge they need; and so on. Insofar as they have objections, those objections consist of temporary discomforts caused by a course that has turned out to be more difficult than they anticipated, a semester in which personal problems divert their attention from academic work, or the constraints on their freedom of choice in the allocation of effort.

A third group of students, and not a small one, consists of those for whom the challenge of course work and grades seems to be too much. They either fail and leave school or work desperately and thereby manage to barely meet minimum requirements. Their college life consists of little beyond academic work; they have no time for other campus activities or, if they engage in them, do so at great risk. Their objections to the present system, if they were voiced, would revolve around the onerousness of the sanctions and the limitations it imposes on their other activities. Many of these students, however, accept the system so completely that they do not question it sufficiently to consider such heresies. They attribute their difficulties to their own failings.

A system that satisfies one of these groups will probably give trouble to another. The system that provides incentive and a reasonable challenge for the middle group will bore the top group and frighten the bottom one. The system that provides sufficient security for the lowest group will seem childlike to the others. What, then, can be done? Is any solution possible? Can students devise a program that will meet the needs of all these types?

We will find no solution if we insist that the same system apply to all students in the same way, that all students be subject to the same rules and the same penalties. But that requirement, after all, probably stems much more from administrative need and custom than from anything else. Systems that could satisfy student criteria might be developed if we removed the restriction that the system apply uniformly to all students. Let us consider what kind of system we might develop for each of the three groups we have described.

The brightest students require a minimal system. They want to be free to pursue knowledge without having to bother with course requirements they regard as trivial. They do not require extrinsic motivations to work at academic tasks (indeed, they sometimes voluntarily impose on themselves far stricter requirements than the university does) and believe themselves quite capable of devising their own challenges, without external support. They do not require relief from academic sanctions nor do they have any problem in freeing time for other pursuits. A system that did away with grades altogether would probably suit them well; it would deprive them of a background of conventional standards to be used in devising their own more difficult variations and, insofar as they participated in organizational activities (as they are likely to do), they would need some substitute for grades as a way of judging others.

Average students would probably want a system like the present one, perhaps with a few changes to make it work more efficiently. The present system does what they want it to, which should not surprise us, since these are the students who have adjusted most satisfactorily to it. They might want changes such as the one a student suggested in an earlier chapter, in which grades would be given in tenths of a point, so that the GPA could reflect even more adequately actual course performance. They would probably want a few escape hatches in the system, by means of which they could occasionally avoid the drastic effect on their GPA of a semester in which their academic load was unavoidably heavy, personal problems affected their ability to work, or they wished to pursue some intellectual interest without fear of penalty. For these purposes, an optional pass-fail feature could perhaps be added to the current system; one might allow students to take certain courses on a pass-fail basis or perhaps allow them, at their option, to take a certain number of semesters under such an arrangement.

The lowest group of students would be hardest to provide for. They require a system that will induce motivation without being too difficult, that will give them knowledge without making them liable to severe penalties in other areas of college life. Perhaps they might be offered a system in which grades were given, but their use would be severely restricted to academic decisions; university officials would not make their grades available to student organizations, to their parents, or to other officials who would base extra-academic decisions on them. Even under such a system, they would suffer from the crippling effects on their self-esteem of less than adequate grades, but we cannot see a way of avoiding that when they simultaneously desire the motivating effects of grades. Perhaps the strict limitation of the bad effects of grades would soften their impact; the student would still have alternative channels of achievement open to him in organizational activity and personal relations, since these opportunities would be unaffected by his grades.

There is an additional difficulty for the students in any such differentiated scheme—it would be difficult to use it to make discriminations among students for organizational purposes. While for many students this would be a distinct advantage, the Kansas student body, when we studied them, relied very heavily on grades in this connection. We would, then, probably create disorganization in the campus social order by introducing such a system (as we would if we did away with grades altogether, as suggested earlier). If grades cannot be used as a standard for making distinctions, what could be used in their place? Would students not have great difficulty establishing a new standard? We think they would have difficulty and have no good suggestions for a replacement. The impact of such a change on campus organization is problematic, and it is in this area that unanticipated consequences, some of them perhaps undesirable (from the point of view of students, faculty, or both), would have to be watched for most closely.

A differentiated system of academic requirements should, for maximum flexibility, allow students to change periodically the plan under which they are enrolled. Incoming students might be counseled, on the basis of achievement test scores and other available information, to take one or another of the options. But, in the end, this should be left to the student's discretion, and he should be able, if he discovers that the plan he has chosen does not suit him, to choose another. This might make for administrative difficulties but, after all, we are considering things from the students' point of view now and from that point of view administration exists to serve students' educational needs and not for its own convenience.

A differentiated system of academic requirements, such as we are proposing as the one students might find most desirable, would have many problems. We have not uncovered all of them here, let alone solved them. But a differentiated system of requirements would, we think, offer the best chance of solving the variety of problems students now have.

STUDENTS AND FACULTY

We have now proposed two different plans for changing the present system of academic requirements, based as it is on grades and the grade point average. From the faculty point of view, we have argued that a complete abolition of grades would effectively accomplish many faculty ends. From the student point of view, we suggested that a differentiated system of requirements in which students could choose a plan ranging from a modified version of the present system to total abolition of grades would best serve their differentiated goals.

Have we, finally, any overall recommendations as to what would be best? No. We think that these decisions will be made in the give-and-take of the political process, as that involves students, faculty, administration, and other interested parties, and not on the basis of the recommendations made by a team of disinterested sociological observers. Furthermore, we are not, of course, disinterested observers. We are faculty members ourselves, and our recommendations would necessarily take as given the interests and goals of that group in any such ultimate proposals. To be specific, our own preference among the plans proposed is for total abolition of grades; as faculty, we think that in the end what would be best for us would be best for the university.

The question might be put somewhat differently. Is there some workable compromise between the two suggested plans? What compromise is workable, of course, depends on the judgments of the parties involved, and to us it seems likely that a great variety of compromises might be reached that would appreciably improve matters, for both faculty and students. A university might, for example, introduce pass-fail procedures slowly, first for a few courses, then for more, increasing the options available to the student periodically. It might abolish grades, except for students who request them.

What is most clear to us is that something ought to be done, for as matters now stand neither faculty nor students achieve their aims.

INDEX